THE RICHEST
REAL ESTATE AGENT

THE
Richest
REAL ESTATE
AGENT

How to Build a Seven-Figure
Business without Sacrificing
Your Relationships

BEN OOSTERVELD

LIONCREST
PUBLISHING

The Richest Real Estate Agent

How to Build a Seven-Figure Business without Sacrificing Your Relationships

ISBN   978-1-5445-2963-9   Hardcover
       978-1-5445-2964-6   Paperback
       978-1-5445-2965-3   Ebook

Contents

Foreword

—By Philip McKernan

Great, yet another how-to book that promises to teach you how to become a millionaire. With, of course, the underlying assumption built in that once you have a thriving business, your life will thrive also. The world does not need any more books, podcasts, events, or YouTube channels screaming this message. You do not need more information that will help you win awards you can use to show the world how great you are. You don't need another book that helps you build a business but ultimately fails to help you build a life.

Ben's approach, however, is refreshingly different. He has learned firsthand the cost of "killing it" in business and how that almost killed his marriage. From his time living on the streets, Ben knows what it's like to live with nothing. He also knows intimately what it feels like to have it all and yet experience the emptiness of losing touch with himself and his family in an obsessive desire for growth, purely for growth's sake.

I too know that journey personally. There was a time when the strongest story in my head was the one telling me that if I made enough money, I would have the freedom to live the life I wanted. It's a story that the logical side of my mind loved, but it was a soul-crushing journey that left me feeling lost, unclear, riddled with self-doubt, and buried in regret. Most real estate training and messaging is built on that archaic and flawed narrative.

Get your license, take the professional profile photo, sign up with a broker, and set your eyes on the goal of becoming number one. Once the marketing is right, it's one straight line to success. The problem is, that game has changed. People want to deal with people with whom they feel a connection, and agents want to be successful at home as well as the office. Who cares if you win awards as a broker and break a million in commission if you find it hard to connect with yourself and others you love? What's the use of being successful if you do not feel satisfied?

What I appreciate most about Ben is that he does the real work to grow as a man, a husband, a father, and a leader. I know this because I vividly remember fighting him on deep patterns and beliefs he held about himself and the world around him. He allowed himself to challenge his thinking and began to reshape his vision of the person he wanted to become. Yes, he wanted to build a successful business using his talents, but he also awoke to the idea of building something special that honored his unique gifts.

Ben's life is not perfect. Perfection does not exist. But it is full of opportunity, excitement, and impact. He's taken his own journey and unpacked it in a deeply intentional way so he could grow. He's redesigned his role as a husband and father and put his business in its place. He's good at helping people grow a real estate business, but his real gift is helping them win the internal award for being the leader they were meant to be. Ben is a unique teacher because he has experienced the pain of insignificance and tasted the beauty of living a life that truly matters.

We are so lucky to get the chance to learn from Ben's wisdom so we can craft a life for ourselves that matters. This book is packed with proven strategies that work on the business side. It will also challenge you to intentionally build a successful business that does not compromise what is truly important to you.

Thank you, Ben, for being so brave.

—Philip McKernan, author and personal coach

Introduction

I t wasn't until my wife told me she wanted to leave me that I finally stopped chasing and started living.

I remember the moment vividly. I was sitting at the backdoor, untying my shoes; I'd just got in. Life seemed great. My coaching business was flourishing and my clients, all real estate agents, were seeing enormous success. Alongside the coaching, my own real estate business was exploding. I became an agent to prove to the industry that there was a better way to sell real estate. Right out of the gate, I won Rookie of the Year. In my first two years, I earned $1.1 million in paid-out commissions. In addition to all of the above, I had started my YouTube channel—this was 2008, before anyone was actually a YouTuber—which was gaining fantastic traction.

Honestly, I was killing it.

I was still untying my shoes, completely unprepared for what was about to unfold, when my wife arrived home. She sat down next to me on the step. "Ben," she said, "I'm done."

For a moment, I didn't understand what she meant. The sentence had come out of nowhere. Did she mean done with us? We'd had terrible fights before, of course, and we'd both said things we didn't mean in the heat of the moment. But this felt different. She wasn't fighting me; we weren't in the middle of an argument. She was telling me softly, sadly, and seriously. When I I looked up at her, I felt like I had been hit by a wrecking ball. She meant it. She was done with our marriage.

I couldn't comprehend what was happening. In my mind, everything I'd done was for her and the kids. I busted my butt so we could have a nice house and nice cars, buy whatever we wanted, take vacations. I told her that. I began to list everything I did for the family, things I believed represented my contribution to the relationship. They were evidence of my value as a man: proof that I was a good provider and protector. What had I done wrong?

My wife told me that I was always chasing something—no matter how good something got, I always wanted more. In the first few years of our marriage, we'd moved ten times. I was always looking for the next big thing. She, meanwhile, was always following in my wake. But, she told me, she couldn't follow anymore. "All the stuff you gave me," she said, "I never wanted it, Ben. I only wanted you."

Her unfiltered honesty and the devastating clarity of her message absolutely destroyed me. Everything in my life always looked awesome. There I was, the big prosperous coach with a truckload of stories about my adventures, triumphs, and successes. Heck, even my family life seemed awesome. Anyone who looked at my social media page would have seen pictures of me taking my kids on dates, spending family time, and generally being an incredible husband and father. That story was mostly true, but no one knew that behind the perfect picture was a lack of true connection. Not even me.

As I digested her words, what destroyed me wasn't what she said. It was the realization that she had been saying it for years and I hadn't listened. When one of my kids asked if they could get a new dad, I couldn't see how seriously he was hurting. I was a steamroller. Anything I wanted, I got. I kept pushing for more and more success. And I wrapped that impulse up in nobility, in *mission*; I told everyone I was doing it for my family.

But the truth was, they didn't want it at all. They tried to tell me as much, but I didn't believe them. I couldn't believe that my wife would want me for who I was, not for how well I performed. I may have always been enough for her, but deep down, I wasn't enough for me.

I remember how that backdoor area looked like it was yesterday. We had five kids, each one of whom had their own cubbyhole for their things. The whole place was a mess, with coats lying everywhere. I lay on the floor in that jumble of stuff, shattered and crying. I kept saying, over and over, *I fucked up, I fucked up.* I truly believed my marriage was over. Later, my wife told me that was the first time she felt that I let my guard down and actually heard her deep anguish and frustration with the lack of connection in our relationship. As I lay there, broken and vulnerable, I remembered leaving rehab years earlier and wanting only two things: a wife who loved me and kids who would come running to the door when I arrived home. I had achieved those goals, and yet I'd lost touch with them.

That wasn't the day my marriage ended. But it was the day I stopped making YouTube videos and made space to work on my marriage. It was the day I realized that $1.1 million, an incredible coaching business, and being a stellar real estate agent would never be enough. Until I was enough.

No Time to Live

If you've picked up this book, my guess is that you will recognize yourself in the story above. Like any real estate agent, you got into this business dreaming of big commission checks, the ability to control your time, and holidays with your family. Your goal was to find freedom, and you believed—correctly—that real estate can be your ticket to freedom.

What you didn't realize is that once you got your license, you would be confronted by a million tasks. Figure out how to find and keep clients. Learn how to list and market homes and deal with buyers. As a real estate agent, your phone is always buzzing. You never reach the end of your to-do list.

By the time you come home at night, all you want to do is grab a beer with your friends or spend time with your kids. But even if you've managed to complete everything on your to-do list, your mind is still racing. *Do I have to book those showings? I should grow my team. Did I get those pictures done? Do I get a stager, should I be doing a mailer, do I door knock, do I hire an assistant?* You're so preoccupied that you're never really present for your life; not at your kid's soccer game, not at your wedding anniversary.

Still, the money is rolling in. The real estate industry says that you should raise your financial goals year after year, so you do. You keep going. You're making money, so you must be doing well, right? The only problem is that you're exhausted all the time. Your service level—the key to why you became successful in the first place—starts dropping. Your energy level is never 100 percent. You're hovering around 60 percent, and then you come home and you have nothing to give to your family. But you give anyway. You power through.

At some point, it gets too much. You decide to hire a buyer's agent to handle sales. But that only causes more problems. Your company grows bigger and there's more work for you to do. You create a mental image of yourself as a procrastinator, as disorganized, when in reality you're running on the spot trying to do five to ten jobs. You tell yourself you'll hire an assistant when you hit a certain number of deals, but by the time you reach that point, you're too busy to hire a team. This dream of freedom isn't playing out like you thought it would. You're hustling all the time just to stay afloat, growing disconnected from the life you originally wanted. You're a tired salesman, not a business owner.

Desperate, you hire a coach. Maybe you take social media courses that you never finish. You try one practical solution after another to transform your business into a well-oiled machine. None of them work. Meanwhile, your clients are leaving because you don't take care of them. You forget to follow up with important clients. Sure, your brand *looks* great, but behind the facade, it's chaos. You're almost cannibalizing your own business. You long for a step-by-step guide, but there's no such thing in this industry.

You know real estate has such high potential to give you the life you want. You just don't know how to get it done.

Here's the hard truth: no practical solution will help you. Your issue is not practical; it is emotional. If this is hard for you to hear, then you probably need to hear it more than you realize. I know because I've been there. I tried so hard to be successful because I believed I was inadequate. I pushed myself so hard that I nearly lost my marriage. That was not a practical problem. It was an emotional issue. If you have a fear of rejection or trauma, if you're a compulsive people pleaser, or if you have other unresolved emotional issues, those tendencies inevitably shape the practical outcomes of your business.

It is impossible to solve an emotional problem with a practical business solution. You have to take a look at your life, get clear on what you want, and get out of your own way. That's how you'll find the freedom you're searching for and unlock the potential of real estate as a career.

The Next Level

I magine the best race car you can create. You can give it the best engine, fit state-of-the-art tires, and install the best possible brakes. But that car is useless without a good driver. It's the same with emotional and practical solutions. As a real estate agent, your mindset and skills are arguably more important than your business structure. This is not to say that coaching or practical training is a waste. It can generate incremental change—maybe move the needle a few percent. But it won't solve your real problems.

So that's where we start—with *you* and what you really want.

So many agents are chasing goals that don't matter to them. They've inherited these dreams from their parents or plucked them from popular culture, but they don't actually want what they *say* they want. It's not their fault. When we're children, no one asks us what we desire: people just tell us. Society, religion, governments—everyone is always telling us what to do.

But you can't achieve a high level of success unless you're certain about where you are heading. Your business strategy won't matter if you're going in the wrong direction. And your financial goal is not your real goal. Imagine you had $20 million in the bank—what then? What life do you want with that money? The money is just a tool to build the life you want, but you have to imagine that life first.

Many times, when I ask agents what they want, they tell me they want to make lots of money. Great. What then? They pause and then describe their perfect days. They want to wake up in the morning and have time to exercise. They want to sit out on the patio and have tea. They look forward to a few more holidays.

Does this sound expensive to you? Because it's not at all. Yet, their financial goal is often in the hundreds of thousands of dollars, if not millions. It's ridiculous: you don't need millions of dollars to sit on a patio and have tea. Why chase such a large financial goal if you don't need that much money? No wonder people struggle to get the level of success they say they want—they don't really want it.

Koukon is a long-standing client of mine and a great example of this. Nowadays, he coaches in my business. But when he first came to me, he was a real estate prodigy—in his early twenties, he was seeing good success with a portfolio of rental properties. Back then, he told me his goal was to take six months a year off and live somewhere else. You might be surprised at how many people have exactly this same goal.

I asked him whether he'd ever tested his desire. Had he taken a month off before? Heck, had he even taken a week? The answer was no. He decided to test out his dream by attending a retreat I was leading with his wife and then staying back an extra week. When he came back to our coaching sessions, the answer was clear: he did not want to travel for six months of the year. Bear in mind that Koukon was building an entire life with this mission in mind, putting massive pressure on himself. And he didn't even want it!

Once you get clear on what you want and find a financial goal that reflects your true desires, you can begin thinking about how to get there. The key to this is energy.

Have you ever had the flu? Imagine yourself lying in bed sick, trying desperately not to puke. Your friend is at the door, dressed in running shoes, asking you to climb a mountain with him. Maybe you've climbed mountains before, but today it's clearly beyond you. No matter how much you wish you could go, you don't have the energy for it. The same principle applies to business. Your skill level, experience, and training matter less than your energy levels.

Part of success is identifying the energy leaks in your professional and personal lives and plugging those leaks. In business, you can conduct a task audit in which you identify the tasks that drain your energy and delegate them to someone else. In your personal life, you can conduct an energy audit. What pulls you down? Are there any stories you're telling yourself, like your body image, that's draining you? Are there relationships in your life that are exhausting? Are you living where you want to live? Not living where you want to can be an enormous energy leak.

Once you've located your energy leaks, you can progress to your inner game. The inner game is about handling the mental blocks that hold you back. It's essential to look at your relationship with your emotions and examine how you talk to yourself in your own head. If you don't tackle these mental blocks, no practical strategy is going to help you.

Once you're clear on what you want, you're running on full energy, and you're getting out of your own way, winning the game is very simple. Now we can deep dive into the short game systems (marketing and sales) and the long game systems (what keeps your clients coming back and referring you for twenty years or more). All agents love shiny new marketing ideas. It's like ice cream—who doesn't want ice cream? But long-game systems are like vegetables: you need them for the strength and nutrients they offer. Sales and marketing may be exciting, but long-game systems keep your client experience at ten out of ten for twenty years. They're what make raving fans and keep them raving.

What You'll Learn in This Book

In these pages, you'll learn how to plot your path to a seven-figure business and, more importantly, how to get out of your own way. This emotional element is essential. Have you ever Googled "how to find clients?" If you do, you'll discover hundreds of millions of strategies. The knowledge to solve any business problem is out there, so why do so many people struggle to find success?

It's because practical solutions aren't the most important element of success—fixing your mindset and your emotional blocks are. This book will help you do that. You'll understand what you really want and how much it will cost, what drains you and fires you up. You'll learn what's holding you back and how to make fear your partner, not your enemy. Through energy audits, you'll discover how to live at optimal energy so that when you get home to your best life, you'll have the energy to enjoy it.

Along the way, we're going to get ridiculously honest, to the point where you may become uncomfortable. But that's good because it means you're growing.

Ultimately, you'll learn how to make a mindset shift from hustler to business owner. We will teach you how to implement the right short-game and long-game processes to skyrocket client experience and build an emotional relationship with your clients. You'll also learn the importance of your long game, built through simple gestures such as remembering birthdays and inspiring closing experiences, and how it can help you keep clients for life. This is not about flash-in-the-pan success. It's about companies that last.

By the time you close this book, you'll know how to create a business that serves you, and not vice versa.

How I Got Here

We all have a story. Whether it's tough and traumatic, like mine, or amazing, it shapes us. Every human being needs to be connected to their backstory. This is mine.

From a very young age, I never knew how to make my parents happy. I broke things. I talked too much. I was hyperactive. I wasn't an easy kid. Yet, what I wanted more than anything was my parents' love.

It wasn't easy to get. My father grew up in challenging circumstances. His father, my grandfather, was imprisoned in a concentration camp and tortured—one of the things his captors did to him was cut off his toes—and it scarred him. He raised my father with little love, and although my dad made improvements on that template, my childhood wasn't ideal. I developed a performance mindset. Love and acceptance were things I *won*, rather than things I got for free.

Sales became my way to win. My dad was a dominant salesman, so selling was my connection to him. Even as a young kid, I excelled at selling. I sold oil changes door to door, Christmas lights, chocolate-covered almonds, everything. Every single sales competition going, I came first. And I didn't just win—I *crushed* the competition.

But sales couldn't fix my sense of inadequacy, and I grew into a tough adolescence. I bounced in and out of jail. I got into fights. I dealt drugs. Ultimately, I ended up in rehab for a year, which was a wake-up call. I needed a reset. When I got out, a head-hunter approached me and offered me a position as a salesperson for Gunnar Office Furnishings, a manufacturing plant that dealt with high-end office furniture for companies. I took the gig. My dad was thrilled.

First day at my job at Gunnar, I was feeling incredible. Perhaps a bit *too* incredible, enough to be cocky, because I marched into the Vice President's office. "Judy," I said—her name was Judy—"what is the most impossible sales goal you can imagine? A goal that I couldn't possibly reach. Tell me, and I'll reach it."

Judy was probably wondering who this young upstart was. I was in my early twenties, no one else in the company was younger than thirty, and this was my first day. But I wasn't done. "I'll meet it," I said, "but if I do, you have to make a deal with me. You have to buy tickets for my entire family to Disneyland."

Judy didn't take the deal—I think she didn't want to buy my tickets—but I met every sales goal anyway. And I kept climbing higher. For the two and a half years I was at Gunnar, I worked my butt off. The only reason I went home at night was because we sold commercial office furniture, and all the people I could sell to closed in the evenings. If we had worked on a twenty-four-hour cycle, I would have worked twenty-four hours and ignored my family. Selling was how I felt good about myself.

During those years, I landed some huge accounts for Gunnar: Husky, Shell Oil, the Calgary City School Board. In the last year I was there, I sold $2.5 million worth of desks. Yet, all I wanted was more. Maybe this was the constant chasing my wife referred to, years later, when she wanted to leave. I was constantly searching for something I couldn't define, pursued by the monster of feeling not quite good enough.

I left Gunnar when I discovered *Rich Dad, Poor Dad* by Robert T. Kiyosaki. I found the audiobook on a CD in the library, which was like Christmas morning for a guy who is dyslexic and struggles with reading. I stuck it into my car and my life changed. I found my tribe of people: entrepreneurs. I couldn't *spell* entrepreneur—still can't—but I knew I belonged with them. I'd always had vision, always loved building things, I loved making money, and I always felt like I never fit in. I had, I felt, the classic makings of an entrepreneur.

In retrospect, the decision to quit Gunnar for real estate investing was foolhardy. I had made $130,000 the previous year selling desks. I was on my way to becoming Gunnar's no. 1 guy, with the potential to earn hundreds of thousands of dollars. But I was filled with blind ambition, so I walked into my President's office—his name was Ron, and he was amazing—and told him I was quitting. I was going to be a real estate investor.

At that point, I owned exactly two houses. One that I lived in and one that I had moved from and was renting out. Not the most stellar investment portfolio. I had no clue how to read a financial statement or analyze investment decisions. Ron shook his head and told me I'd regret this.

He was wrong. And right.

I had no clue how crazy real estate investment would become. In my first two years, in collaboration with investors, I bought forty-one properties. Over seven to eight years, I amassed a portfolio of sixty-one properties. In total, we handled far more houses than that since we bought and flipped several. At one point, I was working in four different cities. Life was good.

Then 2008 came, and the crash hit. Everything crumbled. The stock market collapsed. Financial advisors were committing suicide. Investors were calling me up, desperate to sell their properties so they could stay afloat, and I couldn't sell them; it wasn't possible. I was good at sales, so I'd grown my real estate investing business quickly. But I didn't have any of the long-game processes needed to survive a period like this.

At the time, my family and I had just moved to Hinton, Alberta, a beautiful little town in the mountains. To date, it's one of my favorite places we've lived. My wife and kids took the time to enjoy it, but I experienced none of it. I was working all the time. It was a dark period in my life: I felt completely out of control and overwhelmed. I was in my twenties—nothing had prepared me for such an intense period.

After 2008, I hired a business and life coach, Philip McKernan. I owe so much of the growth in my life to Philip: he challenged the shit out of me, as I now challenge the shit out of my clients. He showed me that I wasn't as backed into a corner as I believed: there were ways to save the business. I just couldn't see them because of the narratives I'd created in my head. Over the course of a year, we liquidated several of my properties, sold them to investors, and repositioned the whole company. I ended up holding nine properties and redesigning my life.

I started by coaching small businesses, which took off. Initially, my focus was on sales and marketing, but this quickly narrowed to personal development. I worked with all kinds of clients—energy companies, videographers, entrepreneurs, investors—but ultimately, I niched into real estate agents. Why? Because I realized they needed coaching more than anyone else: absolutely none of them were actually running a business, and most were flirting with burnout or financial desperation.

Here's an example of how low service standards are in the real estate industry. When I was still an investor, I did a deal for sixteen condos with a few other investors. All the condos were listed with one real estate agent. As she showed us around, I began calculating her commission. Assuming she earned $5,000 a pop, she picked up almost $100,000 worth of commission on that one sale. For two weeks of work. I was a pretty big fish at the time and it was so easy for her to make $100,000. Yet, she didn't even send me a thank-you card, never mind tickets to Disneyland for my whole family. That's when I realized that if I became a real estate agent, I would absolutely dominate the game.

The whole real estate industry was teaching real estate agents to chase sales, not build businesses. There was a lack of focus on how to keep a client for twenty years. Everything was about the next transaction.

The agents I coached became very successful very quickly. More importantly, they *stayed* successful. Any coach can come into your life and give you a boost, but it's important to me to create lasting impact.

I'd been a business coach for years. As I decided to niche into real estate, I thought, *what would it be like if I did the work as well as coaching?* I convinced twelve real estate agents to join a program called the Real Estate Start-up Program. I rented a room from the

Edmonton Real Estate Board to coach once a week. The idea was that these clients would see me do the work they were hoping to do; I would become a real estate agent they could emulate. I would lead with a shovel, by their side, every step of the way. We would be in it together.

Within a year of becoming an agent, I won Rookie of the Year. Not by a small margin—by a ton. I had zero lead gen, barely had a website, and had almost no business cards. Yet, I landed $440,000 in paid-out commissions that first year. The next year, that number jumped to $660,000. That's a total of $1.1 million in commissions. By the third year, I led the top real estate team in all of western Canada, all while running retreats, doing keynote talks, leading a high-end business mastermind, traveling five to six times per year, and being a dad to five kids and a husband to a beautiful wife.

After eight years, with both businesses growing, I decided to sell my real estate company and give up my license. I'm doubling down on coaching because I see so many people chase money when they're actually chasing a feeling. And it's ruining their lives. The real estate world isn't healthy. More families are breaking up. Divorce is spiking. There's more drinking happening and more cheating. All because agents are chasing a financial goal they may not even want. They're running after somebody else's dreams.

So I'm on a mission. I'm going to change this industry and help real estate agents make this amazing business their servant rather than their master. Along the way, I'm going to help them uncover who they really are. One of the best things about being a coach is that I get to help people work through their emotional blocks.

The American dream is a staple of North American life: we're told we can get anything we want. Everyone wants freedom and success, but 90 percent of us don't achieve it because we self-sabotage. We don't know how to develop a relationship with our emotions; all we want is to feel happy. When we do feel bad, we bury it and it starts expressing itself as triggers, self-sabotage, and bad decisions. The American dream is real, but it has to start *within* you. You can be happy today, not in some distant future.

I can help. Thanks to my backstory, when I look at someone, I can see their pain and what is holding them back. I can help them overcome it. As a child who didn't get what he needed, as a street kid who hurt every day, as a man who tried suicide, and as a husband whose wife almost left him, there's so much I've overcome. It's shaped me, and I truly believe I have the keys to help people grow and live a thriving and successful life filled with happiness, connection, and—why not?—a big bank balance. Creating that change is what drives me.

I'm coming at this as a man who has already won the game. I've got a family that loves me. My office looks directly at the ocean. I live in one of the most beautiful neighborhoods in the world, on West Vancouver. I drive the car I want to drive. I hang out with people I want to hang out with. I get to sit on my patio and have tea if I want. I get to contribute to a lot of people's lives. I'm no longer that man who was chasing. I'm willing to let go of anything that does get in my way. And I'm still on my own journey, watching my reactions, watching my triggers, understanding what's in my way—I'm a student of my own work.

So let me tell you, as someone who has walked this path, real estate is one of the best businesses in the world—*if done right.* It can give you the freedom that you've wanted to connect more with people that you love and to live an adventurous life. You just have to become a business owner, not a hustler, and get clear on what you want. Then you can make your business serve you.

How to Tell
Whether This Book Is for You

This book is a guide to aligning your business life with the life you want to live, designed around your genuine values. It shows you how to create a company that serves your true goals.

It is a personal growth manual to help real estate agents level up their emotional intelligence and develop a business owner mindset. It will show you how to use emotional connections in branding and marketing to create deeper relationships with clients, relationships that are not based purely on performance. You'll learn how to keep clients for twenty years and more and have them referring you to their friends on an ongoing basis.

This book is also a curated guide to systems that you will actually use. It cuts through the hundreds of ways to build a real estate business and provides a simple framework you can execute very easily today.

This isn't your typical real estate book filled with get-rich-quick schemes or meaningless ego boosts. There is no "how to be successful overnight" strategy because the real game is not about flash-in-the-pan success. I want to help you build out your long game and put in place systems that will stand the test of time. This is more about your mindset, beliefs, and connecting with who you are to build a long-lasting company.

This book is also not about me telling you I've done everything right. In no way am I saying, "I used these systems and achieved success; follow them and you can be like me!" That never works. This is the biggest problem with most real estate books: there's always some successful agent preaching about how you can turn into him. If you try to become like me, you will fail. If I try to become like you, I will fail. You need to be you and find success that matches your terms.

Which is why this is not a copy-and-paste guide taken from Google that tells you about new ways of marketing yourself. It's heavy on personal development and doing the hard work to build a real business. And it applies well beyond real estate—these lessons can be applied to any business. Ultimately, it's a simple framework based on human connection and sound systems that are designed to get you what you want.

Last, this book is not complicated. It's a lot like losing weight. We all know how to lose weight: eat less, exercise more. Simple, right? Yet, so many people struggle with their weight. The how is easy, but execution isn't. The how is this book and it's very simple—as simple as picking up the phone and calling a client on a consistent basis. That's the point. We overcomplicate everything. Hopefully, this book will help you unwind the areas where you hold yourself back so you can finally execute on the very simple things it takes to build a seven-figure business.

The Seven-Figure Mindset

When I started out as an entrepreneur, I set a financial goal of earning $6,000 per month. I thought that if I could bring in six grand, I would be set. Today, this number looks ridiculously low to me. However, it was what I believed feasible then.

Fast forward a few years. I was sitting in my office, calculating receipts for the month. When I arrived at the final figure, I stared at it in disbelief. Then I called up my wife.

"Renee," I said, breathlessly, "we just made $50,000."

We couldn't believe it. Fifty grand! It was like winning the lottery. Some part of me thought it was a fluke, but it wasn't. We earned fifty grand the following month and the month after that. Some months, we even touched a hundred grand.

During that period of wild growth, my mindset shifted. I quickly forgot my paltry six-grand goal and became used to my newfound wealth. Fifty grand landing in my bank account each month wasn't surprising anymore. It was normal; I expected it.

Although my financial capacity had leveled up, however, my inner game hadn't. The money was great, but it didn't alter my fundamental beliefs about myself or resolve my emotional issues. It felt like a huge win, but it didn't convince me that I was a winner.

And so, instead of leveling up to match my financial success, I leveled down to match my self-perception. I sabotaged myself.

I've done this three or four times in my career, so I know that self-sabotage follows a clear pattern. First, I would grow the business to new heights, taking myself and my family to the brink of the next level. I'm talking here about generational wealth; the kind of money that would have ensured the security of my children. While my business was growing externally, however, I was still battling negative narratives about myself. Inadequate. Procrastinator. Undeserving. I was still chasing my father's love, trying to prove myself because nothing I did gave me the message that I was enough.

What did I do? I made silly decisions, jeopardizing the success of my business and my family's security in pursuit of nebulous goals. I used money set aside to pay taxes to buy a new house, insisting that more would flow in to make up the shortfall. It didn't. I insisted we move, ostensibly to access better opportunities but really in a quest for something new, something different, that would scratch the itch for more. So I uprooted myself and my family and we started again in a new town, which set us back.

I fiddled with business processes that already worked flawlessly. I aimed for foolhardy and unnecessary targets. Each of these missteps undermined my progress, cost valuable energy, and set me back. I was still doing pretty well, but not as well as I should have been. All the while, I was trying to fill unmet emotional needs by altering my external circumstances. It was the endless chasing my wife spoke about on the day she almost left me, the cycle that wouldn't end and allow me to simply *be*.

Looking back, it's clear that I pushed so hard because, on a fundamental level, I didn't believe I deserved so much success. That $6,000 goal I had as a young entrepreneur wasn't just a number—it was a representation of what I believed I deserved. When I earned more than that, my psyche rebelled.

I didn't know this consciously, of course. Consciously, I was very happy to see $50,000 drop into our bank account. But on a subconscious level, I didn't believe I was worth that money because my internal value didn't match my financial value. So every time the company got ahead, I would drag it back. Self-sabotage became my glass ceiling.

Your Self-Worth Is Your Net Worth

P hilip McKernan, my mentor for many years, has a saying: "Your net worth is always tied to your self-worth." Write that down and stick it on your bathroom mirror. If you have a home office or a desk you consistently sit at, put it there. Tape it anywhere you can read it every single day, because this one line is the foundation to long-lasting success.

Many real estate agents enjoy a few big years, pulling in millions of dollars in annual revenue, before losing their way and their income. They go through a feast-and-famine cycle, earning millions one year and almost nothing the next. Real estate coaches will tell you that breaking that cycle and maintaining your success is about consistency, discipline, and the right systems. I agree—partially. Those things matter, but they're not the *foundation* of your success. The foundation is your self-worth. If your self-worth and your financial success don't match, you will make them match, even if that means self-sabotage.

I'm living proof. I went from imagining that I could earn $6,000 a month to bringing in $100,000 a month, but I still felt like the six-thousand-dollar guy. My subconscious was telling me, *you're not worth that kind of money. You don't deserve it. You think you're going to level up again? Give me a break. You're a joke.* These narratives spun in my head until I destroyed what I had built. I couldn't help myself. I didn't know I was doing it.

I only progressed when I worked through my demons and my emotional friction. And by "progress," I don't mean earning a hundred thousand grand for one month or two. I mean earning that much every month for a *year*, before scaling up to a hundred and fifty thousand. That's progress: attaining a level of success that you can *sustain* and then growing from there to the next level.

To achieve that, your self-esteem *must* align with the numbers in your bank account. In order to stay successful, you have to marry your net worth and your self-worth. Once you do that, earning will be easy. You won't be chasing money anymore—it will be chasing you.

But to get there, you need to fix your internal game. You need to grow a seven-figure mindset.

The Seven-Figure Mindset

I n the past few years, "mindset" has become an overused term. It seems like every coach, entrepreneur, or financial guru is always talking about "mindset," to the degree that the word has lost its meaning. Let's step back from jargon for a minute, and I'll explain exactly what I mean.

Imagine an entrepreneur. He dreams of owning a chain of restaurants. He starts with one and focuses on making it successful. He creates the menu, hires the staff, does a big launch, works on keeping his customers happy. He spends countless nights balancing the accounts and building relationships with the community. It's hard work—every day, he hustles to move toward his dream of owning a successful chain of restaurants. More and more people become repeat customers. People in his community recognize and appreciate him. He has enough revenue to open another restaurant, then another, and yet another.

Over many years, he builds his dream into a reality. By his mid-fifties, he's the proud proprietor of a $10-million chain of restaurants, built with his blood, sweat, and tears. He no longer needs to work: he has fantastic processes in place, allowing the company to run like a well-oiled machine. He keeps working not because he must but because he enjoys it. Maybe he takes a more hands-off approach for a while and works from a beach somewhere beautiful. He goes on vacations and spends time with his family.

He's built a business that serves the life he's dreamed of having, and he's living that life. Unreservedly and with happiness. He knows he deserves it.

At the age of seventy, he feels ready to disengage fully from the business and transition to enjoying his retirement. He ponders the future of his business and selects an heir. Maybe it's one of his children, a nephew or niece, or a trusted family friend.

Whoever they are, they inherit an exceptionally successful business. The company is still a well-oiled machine. Our owner has worked hard to build smooth, effective systems. The business almost runs itself. The new owner, however, lacks the abundant seven-figure mindset. He thinks more like an employee than a business owner. He has played no part in its success and isn't used to earning so much money. He doesn't feel like he deserves it.

What do you think happens?

This story may be hypothetical, but I'm pretty sure you've heard of real businesses like this. Someone builds a hugely successful business from the ground up, passes it to an heir, and within a few years, it's much less successful. In the worst-case scenario, maybe it's even bankrupt. Why? What's happening here?

The founder, who built the business from the ground up, grew with it over the years. He adopted what I call a seven-figure mindset. His mindset reflected his knowledge, his self-worth, and the value of the business. The person who inherited it, however, had a much less expansive mindset—let's say a $200,000 mindset. The business shrank under the heir's stewardship not because they lacked skills or experience but because their mindset didn't match the company's value. So the business started to reflect their internal value.

The moral of this story is not hustle and hard work. The heir also worked hard for the company and hoped it would prosper. The moral of the story is that *hustle and hard work will only take you so far*. Hustle can bring you success, but mindset and internal value will keep you successful.

If you don't believe me, consider the opposite scenario. What would happen if you gave a $200,000 business to our original owner, the one who created a chain of restaurants from scratch? He would do again what he has done before—he would quickly grow it into a seven-figure business because he has a seven-figure mindset.

Here's what drives me crazy about real estate coaching: most coaches focus on getting the next sale and measure success mostly by volume of transactions. Coaches always talk about prospecting, door knocking, lead gen, the best software, the best systems, buyer agents. Their process is designed to make clients "successful," but they're totally focused on one metric—namely, sales or winning new clients. If we dig into what most real estate coaching is about, we'll quickly realize that it's more about sales coaching than true business coaching.

In my opinion, hustle and sales are great when you're starting out. Once you get going, however, they do not lead to sustainable success and real freedom. Once you have sales, then what? How do you stay successful? The thinking that got you your first sales is not the thinking that will bring you long-term success.

The answer to the question is mindset. Mindset is arguably the most important factor in sustaining success. Think about it. You are the person running the team and making the decisions. The whole business operates through the filter of you. But no one is teaching *you* how to level up. They simply assume it will happen or, worse, that your inner growth is not a significant factor in the success of your business. But if you don't grow your personal value in tandem with your business, you're not going to sustain your newfound wealth.

What Holds You Back

The opposite of a seven-figure mindset is, of course, a limiting mindset. Unfortunately, this is what most real estate agents display when I start working with them. Once you break out of your limiting habits of thinking, there's no ceiling to what you can achieve.

A limiting mindset comes in many flavors, and what holds you back depends on the unique cocktail of your psychology. It's built of your fears, your backstory, and the narratives that drive you. I can't cover every possible limiting belief in these pages, but let's go through three of the most common, all of which I see regularly in the real estate industry. Each of these thought processes is a common symptom of a narrow mindset and will limit how much you can grow as a real estate agent.

"I don't need help"

When I coach a class, I often ask the crowd, *How many of you love to receive help?* Maybe one or two hands go up in the audience, but that's about it. Then I ask, *how many of you struggle to ask for help?* Suddenly, almost every hand in the room shoots up.

If this is your attitude, it's not your fault. From an early age, we're taught to idolize hard work. We learn that we must make it on our own. Our education systems measure individual merit and discourage collaboration. Do you know what they call collaboration in school? Cheating. We're programmed to work alone and to believe that if we receive help, our achievements are less praiseworthy.

This is where the hustle mentality stems from. If you learn to be a lone wolf, you will work yourself to the bone before you ask for help. Don't get me wrong, you can hit certain milestones this way. But if you want to be extraordinary—if you're looking to build a seven-figure company—then you can't do it on your own. You will need help. More importantly, you will need a mindset that lets you receive help.

"Discipline is everything"

Hard work isn't the only thing we idolize; we love discipline. I can't count the number of clients who've told me they are procrastinators, or disorganized, or lazy. The problem, they tell me, is their lack of discipline. If they just had more discipline, they'd get it done.

Discipline is great, but it's not the answer. It is a very aggressive, low-energy way of getting ahead.

Think of it this way. I have a son whose room is always messy. I tell him, *You need to wake up half an hour early every day and clean your room before school.* It's a good system, right? The room gets tidied every day, he doesn't have much opportunity to make it messy again, and it doesn't interfere with his activities or homework.

Now, if you are a parent, you know this plan is a disaster. What kid is going to give up half an hour of sleep to clean a room he doesn't think is messy in the first place? I can insist he does it, of course. I can tell him discipline is an important life skill and he must learn it. But it's such low motivation that it's unsustainable. *I* wouldn't do it.

Now, say I announce to my son that we're going to Disneyland in the morning. I need him to clean his room this evening, though, so that it's neat for when he comes back. Do you think he'll do it? Of course! He won't sleep the whole night from excitement anyway, and now cleaning his room is associated with a trip he actually cares about.

It's not discipline that's the problem. It's your motivation. Real estate agents who constantly yell at themselves for being "lazy" are not looking at the real issue: they are not lazy; they simply don't want to do the tasks, just like my son didn't really want a clean room. Part of developing a seven-figure mindset is understanding what truly motivates you and what business you want.

"I just need to know how"

How to run a real estate business is no longer a secret. If you Google it, you'll find thousands of articles, great training videos, and fool-proof tips. You know the Bible phrase "Ask and it shall be given." Google fulfills that promise.

It's no surprise, then, that most real estate agents already know how to run their business. Yet, they still obsess over not achieving what they want, convincing themselves that their processes are at fault. In an effort to become the best, they become paralyzed.

But in doing so, they massively overestimate the importance of the how. Have you ever researched how to get a six-pack? Let's be honest: most of us have. Google is full of diet plans, exercises, and step-by-step videos. Yet, most of us still have mum and dad bods. Why? Because knowing *how* to get a six-pack isn't enough. You still need to execute.

Execution rests on mindset, not on brutal discipline. You won't get a six-pack by shouting at yourself to buck up and berating yourself for not abstaining from sugar for eighty days. Those actions will just make you hate yourself. When you raise your personal value, however, you will lose weight. When you can say to yourself, *I deserve to be twenty pounds lighter* and mean it, you'll take the action that gets you there.

Obsessing over the how is part of a limiting mindset. When you shift your value and attain a seven-figure mindset, you'll learn to move beyond those surface-level issues to access what is really holding you back.

Meaningful change comes from first shifting your mindset and fixing your internal value. Once you do that, your real estate systems—your how—will fall into place. That is why I'm writing this book. This isn't a "how-to" book; you've got hundreds of those. This is a book to change how you view yourself and your belief systems, tapping into your potential on a fundamental level.

Sabotage and Self-Awareness

The seven-figure mindset features in the first chapter of this book because it is the foundation to everything you do. Later in the book, we'll discuss all the systems, tactics, and frameworks you need. But if I give them to you now, without helping you shift your mindset, what will you do with them? Not much, probably. Before long, you'll be looking for the next tactic. That's why mindset comes first. Everything else sits on this bedrock.

If you take just one lesson from this book, let it be this: *mindset is everything.* Consider two real estate agents: let's call them Steve and Greta. Both of them have been in the game for a while and know how to run their companies. They're using similar tactics. Yet Steve is seeing far more success than Greta. Why?

It's simple: Greta self-sabotages because she hasn't fixed her internal game. She doesn't believe she is worthy of success, so she pushes it away.

Self-sabotage expresses itself in the most unexpected ways. Have you ever met a real estate agent who keeps switching brokerages? They always have fantastic reasons. *I don't have the support. I don't have the training.* But no brokerage is ever enough, and they never stop switching. This happens because the brokerage isn't the problem. The problem is their mentality. Their sense of inadequacy tells them the solution to their problems lies in altering external circumstances.

Another example of self-sabotaging behavior is entering into inappropriate partnerships. So many real estate agents partner with someone not because they want a teammate but because they're lonely. They're tired of striking out on their own, so they fill a social need with a business proposition.

This is obviously a terrible idea. What the real estate agent *should* do is go out and make friends. They should join a hiking group or socialize at a party. They *shouldn't* split their business with someone because they need to connect to other human beings. But so many agents do, and soon they're giving away half their money to a partner who doesn't do their fair share. It's self-sabotage.

Mindset and self-worth are complex topics, and delving into them in detail will take a whole book. But I hope I've shown how crucial it is that you understand your emotions, your backstory, and your beliefs because they contribute to your mindset and your mindset contributes to your success. If you want to win the real estate game, you *must* be self-aware. You must get clear on who you are and what you're avoiding. Burying your negative thoughts and emotions doesn't work because that is where the self-sabotage hides.

I'm not saying you have to fix yourself completely before you step into the office. Internal growth is an ongoing process, and issues don't disappear with a wave of a wand. But you have to be at peace with both your strengths and weaknesses. You have to be willing to see yourself clearly because only then will you be able to understand your motivations and check your actions. That's the key to gargantuan success: self-awareness and self-acceptance.

Once you start working on your internal game, you'll soon grow the seven-figure mindset. Agents with this mindset accept winning because they see it as normal. Every move they make is viewed through the prism of this success and the knowledge that they deserve it. They act with confidence, without fighting themselves. They have systems that support them, and they know how to get out of their own way. They trust themselves.

But you can't fake this attitude. You can't look in the mirror and tell your reflection, *Wow! You're an amazing agent!* and suddenly shift your negative self-perception. This doesn't work. In fact, it holds you back. Here's why: when you stand in front of the mirror and say those words, you're trying to generate a feeling. But you don't actually *feel* like this. Once your mind notices the gap between what you're saying and feeling, it will default to the original belief.

When you have a seven-figure mindset, success comes naturally and easily, as an extension of your self-belief. You act in the way successful people act because you *are* successful, not because you're trying to prove something to yourself or others. Here's a great test. Agents with a limiting mindset act from a place of scarcity. They choose their marketing based on how cheap it is because they expect to lose that money. They see it as a cost, rather than an investment.

Agents with a seven-figure mindset, however, expect to win with their money. They buy the best marketing, no matter what it costs, because it is an investment. If $20,000 worth of marketing can win them $60,000 worth of business, that's a great return. They make their decisions expecting to profit from them.

No One Loves a Winner—
except You

G rowing a seven-figure mindset is not about tactics or systems. It's about understanding your emotions, narratives, and backstory. You must tap into the power of self-awareness, accept yourself, and shake off your limiting beliefs. You must create an emotional mindset that matches your financial goals so that you can marry your net worth and your self-worth. Success should no longer feel like a happy surprise or a one-in-a-million chance—it must become normal.

This is the key to achieving what you want and keeping it.

It took me years to understand this. Again and again, I sabotaged myself because I refused to examine my feelings or thoughts. When I finally analyzed what held me back, I found a limiting belief from my childhood that tainted how I approached life.

I was raised in a strict Christian family, where my parents often quoted the Bible. One quote I heard over and over again was, "It's easier for a camel to pass through the eye of a needle than it is for a rich man to get into heaven."

Stop there for a second. Read that again. A camel has to *squeeze* through the eye of a needle before anyone with wealth would see heaven. Well, I was earning fifty to a hundred grand a month, so I was definitely wealthy. Logically, that meant I was going to hell.

I don't think that's what the Bible is trying to teach, but it is definitely what I internalized as a child. Subconsciously, I demonized money. As much as I desired it, I believed—somewhere, tucked away into the recesses of my mind—that it was ruining me. So every time I made more cash, I sabotaged it.

When I finally identified that limiting belief, I had to exorcise it. Was this what I believed, or was it something I had been told? When I examined it, I found that I like having money. I deserve it. I can be wealthy and still be a good person. Nowadays, other people's opinions don't matter to me—neither praise nor criticism. I'm enough for myself and for the most important people in my life. I no longer need to prove anything to my father.

As you'll discover when you become successful, This kind of internal security is essential when you reach the top. Society tends not to love those who win all the time. We all prefer to cheer for the underdog. In the National Hockey League in the late '90s, the Detroit Red Wings were the team to beat. Year after year, I wanted them to fail. I hoped they'd score in their own net. I secretly hoped their goalie pulled a muscle so they had to use a backup. When one of their team members sustained an injury, I cheered and hoped it meant someone else would have a shot at winning the Stanley Cup.

You know why I did this? Because I knew the feeling of being an underdog. I've been there. I know the pain of not winning. But it takes a completely different mindset to be the Detroit Red Wings and win the Stanley Cup year after year. Some people supported them, of course. Their tribe. Outside their tribe, everyone wanted to see them fall flat on their face. When you win, the only people who will cheer for you will be your tribe.

To grow a seven-figure mindset, you must make peace with that. As you keep winning, you're going to trigger people who want the same success as you but can't get it. They will dislike you, reject you. Be prepared for some people to actively root against you.

I learned this the hard way. I was young, pumped with my success; I had no clue how some people saw me or what kind of psychological impact I had on them. I didn't know people didn't cheer for winners. I remember going to a family member's house one day for dinner. This guy was a friend. As I helped him wash the dishes, we were chatting, and I said innocently, "Can you believe I made $70,000 this month?" It was the first time I'd hit that target and I was in awe. I wasn't trying to boast; I just wanted to share the good news. I thought he would be happy for me.

That one statement had a huge negative impact on our relationship. For the rest of the day, he went into a negative spiral. He started expressing resentment toward his family and taking his frustrations out on them. It reached a point where I had to step in and pull him away from the negativity he was spewing at his own kids. After that, we didn't speak for two years.

When you grow your seven-figure mindset, you can achieve the success you deserve. But be prepared; you may need to stand alone. Know what you want, and keep a small tribe of people who trust you and genuinely want to see you succeed.

Today, I live every day expecting money and opportunities to come my way. I no longer feel guilt or shame about being successful. Nonetheless, I keep an eye out for my shadow. I grew up insecure and convinced I was inadequate. Some days, I still wake up feeling like a loser. But I don't give those emotions the power to cripple me anymore. I just greet them, thank them for reminding me where I come from, and wave them goodbye. And they leave.

It has made me stronger. I'm at peace now with someone rejecting me, with failure or criticism, because deep down I know who I am. That's the secret.

2

Setting Your Compass

E arly in my career, I was a wunderkind. I regularly set and met gigantic goals. I sold $2.5 million worth of office furniture at Gunnar Office Furnishings, landed the largest clients in the city, and then quit to invest in real estate and amassed forty-one properties in fourteen months—all while I was still in my twenties.

But that didn't begin to touch the true depths of my ambitions. I wanted to own a thousand properties. I dreamed of one day owning the Edmonton Oilers of the NHL. Nothing was enough.

In the eyes of others, I was a man who knew what he wanted and where he was going. As a society, we *love* large goals. We put them on a pedestal and praise the determination to achieve them. But how often do we stop and ask *why* we feel a need to achieve so much? As I strove for more, I didn't stop to consider what was driving me.

It was only when I struggled with my business and found myself in the throes of burnout that I stopped to consider what I was doing.

I could no longer find the motivation to reach the targets I had set myself. Even worse, I never felt happy. No matter what I achieved, my emotions never matched my success. I was forced to examine what I really wanted and why.

The answers shocked me. I discovered that my huge goals stemmed from a place of inadequacy and a sense of emotional lack, which I traced back to my relationship with my father. He was a top salesman who respected hustle. I joined the same profession, with the intention of dominating the game and showing him what I could do. Each time I won, I felt like he noticed me. When he noticed me, I felt loved. This feeling fed my desire to achieve more and more, until I drove myself to exhaustion.

From the outside, I looked like I had it all together. Internally, however, my objectives didn't reflect the life I truly wanted to live; they were shaped by my subconscious and by emotions I refused to look at. Those emotions were driving the show, propelling me unconsciously where they wanted to take me.

If you had told me this was happening, I would have dismissed you. I might even have fought you. I was convinced the dreams I cherished were mine alone. Yet, the longer I chased these gargantuan and inauthentic desires, the more complicated my life became.

The truth is, what I wanted was very simple. When I left rehab, I was grateful to be alive and not in jail. I felt a deep clarity about what mattered to me in life: a wife who loved me, kids who ran to the door when I came home, and a life that was filled with fun and adventure. *This* was the life I really wanted. I couldn't see how the goals I set myself were driving me in the opposite direction.

Discover Your Own Goals

Building a seven-figure business is hard. You will be kicked in the teeth. You will face insurmountable obstacles. There will be times you bury your face in your hands and wonder, why the heck did I start this?

Persevering with the business owner's journey requires lots of strength and lots of energy. It's much harder to muster these if, at heart, you're chasing someone else's goals. Even if you succeed and build that seven-figure business you're craving, it will be much harder to sustain if you don't have a deep understanding of why you're doing it.

Business planning seminars often ask you how much money you want to make. They very rarely ask why. The assumption is that you have a plan and know what that plan costs. But this is rarely accurate. The truth is, most of us don't know what we truly desire. We follow society's guidance or the paths our parents have mapped out, without asking ourselves what matters to us. Sometimes, like me, we let childhood pain and unprocessed emotions dictate our actions. None of these approaches will fulfill us.

To build the life you want, you must know what you want. To do that, you will need to dig into your emotions and find out. Have you ever seen a business plan that deals with emotions or emotional intelligence? Most likely not. Yet, time and again, these override more practical concerns. The most profound conversations I have with my clients are not about processes or practical problems. They are about self-sabotage and making decisions that don't serve them. Why? Because they're working with unresolved emotions and allowing the subconscious to drive their behavior. If you ignore your emotions, they will haunt your decisions.

This is why you must examine your emotions, work through your feelings, and connect with your honest desire. Set your compass to what you truly want to achieve. If you don't, even an iron-clad business plan can't help you.

Find the Life You Want—Then Live It

Sometimes it seems as though there's always someone trying to tell us what to do. Parents, religion, governments—everyone has a blueprint for the best way to live our lives. Sometimes those blueprints are so appealing that we happily adopt them as our own.

A big house, a loving family, lots of money and social status? Sure, sounds great.

But when we adopt someone else's blueprint, there's always a cost. We don't discover what *we* want. It's only natural: no one asks us what we want, so we never learn to ask ourselves. Typically, instead of examining our psyche and exploring our desires, we use money as a scorecard.

Don't get me wrong—making money is great. But your financial goals must serve what you love. If they don't, they will be unfulfilling and hollow. The real estate industry is full of agents suffering from burnout. They're chasing monetary goals that aren't backed by purpose or intention. Instead, they're looking for an emotional fix. Amassing wealth is a way to feel secure, to convince ourselves we're doing the right thing. But when our financial goals aren't connected to our authentic desires, the money doesn't have the desired effect. When we reach one goal, we instantly set our sights on another. No amount is enough.

The real estate industry actively advocates this trajectory: we're taught to grind and hustle, but we're never taught to ask why. This approach leads to burnout and broken relationships. Even those agents who do achieve monetary success purely through hard work and hustle can still be left unhappy. They want a connection with their family or the freedom to take a day off without pressure. They ask me, *Ben, how do I build a business that doesn't eat into my time, take away evenings with my family, or interrupt the adventures I've always wanted?* I'll tell you what I tell them: chasing money is not the answer.

The secret to real success is asking yourself, *what do I want?* What fires you up and gives you shivers down your spine when you think about it? What activity keeps you awake from anticipation and excitement? When I ask clients these questions, most of them know the answers—they just haven't looked at those answers because they're convinced they need to focus purely on the "practical." I talk to people who love to play an instrument, but they don't learn because they think they can't afford to take time off from work. I meet folks who adore race cars but would never aspire to buy one because they think it's a stupid goal. Others long to write or paint or draw, but they don't because there's no monetary value attached to doing those things.

How many genuine desires have you buried because you didn't want to feel as though you were being foolish with your money or because they didn't serve your financial goals or advance your career? How many sides of yourself have you locked away because they seem frivolous?

Those desires are what make life worth living. They're your real goals, your real wants. You need them in your life because they are your fuel. They are actually what life is about. You don't need millions of dollars to have the life that you want. Nobody does. You *do* need to do what you love because that *is* the life you want.

If you delay your dreams, you will die with regrets. You will regret not taking that trip to Machu Picchu, or showing your wife the Grand Canyon, or standing up on that stage and reciting your poetry. You may even die divorced because you didn't invest time in your relationships. You want to know the secret to a fulfilling life? You fucking live *today*. That's it—that's the secret. You can start living 1 percent of your dream: buy those hockey skates or write that novel or buy those hiking boots—anything. But you have to start. Because if you're not doing what you can to actively live the life you want to live today, it will never expand so that you're living it all the time.

If you don't set your compass, you'll be left with the markers of fulfillment society offers you: a big bank account, a holiday home, maybe vacations with people you don't connect with. How lame is that? Start living today. Do the things that light you up. When you play that guitar, or sing that song, or drive that car, you feel *alive*. You become a better spouse, parent, friend, and boss. You become magnetic—and you can bet your life that will have an impact on your business. But if you don't live today, you will burn out, having pushed through your days deeply unhappy. I promise you that.

One of my coaching clients was the owner of a Royal LePage brokerage, a hugely successful business. As part of my coaching program, I introduced him to the concept of "Set Your Compass." Then I asked him to do one thing that did not meet his financial goals but fed his soul.

He didn't even have to think about it: he knew exactly what he wanted to do. For decades, he'd harbored a secret desire to sing, but he never did because he was scared of looking stupid. On the outside, his life and company looked fantastic; I'm sure many people admired him. But on the inside, he wasn't happy. He wasn't doing anything that energized him. He wasn't living.

It took courage for him to learn how to sing. For so long, he had told himself that singing didn't matter. He had to fight through the resistance his mind was giving him. But he took the first small step: he booked a singing coach.

Most coaching courses focus primarily on business plans. I understand why. A business plan is a trajectory toward success, and I love creating them. There is nothing more exciting to me as an entrepreneur than solving business problems and making money, and a business plan is a concrete expression of those values. But for business plans to really work, they must include emotional needs.

Think about my client. I could have worked on his business plan for months and created a list of financial targets, but it wouldn't have solved his essential problem: he was unhappy. He needed a fuel source, an activity that energized him and gave him purpose. Singing was that activity: it was an emotional need. We have to include emotional needs in our business plan so we can pay attention to them and nurture them. Once we do, not only will we know what activities make life worth living, but we will also tackle the self-sabotaging behaviors and emotional frictions that disrupt our business. I didn't pay attention to my emotional needs for years, and I ended up chasing gargantuan goals that had nothing to do with what I loved or the life I wanted. Don't follow the same path I did—or if you're already on it, choose another one.

This is crucial: paying attention to your emotional needs is what it takes to win. No professional sportsperson will come to their game drunk or at less than optimal health. Business is a game. If you're not emotionally sound or emotionally ready for the game, it doesn't matter how good your business plan is—you can't win. Not at your business and not in your life.

Years after my client started singing, he came on a retreat with me and a few others. At one point, as we sat around a campfire, he stood up and sang for us. He was petrified, but he did it. And let me tell you, it was beautiful. We had goose bumps.

Find out what fuels you and build your compass around it. Then start living it, today.

Exercise: Five Happiest Days of Your Life

To discover what fuels you—what should be the foundation of your life—I recommend an exercise called the Five Happiest Days of Your Life. This exercise was created by Philip McKernan.

On paper, it looks like the easiest exercise in the world, but it is remarkably hard to complete. Ready? Here's what you do:

Write down the five happiest days of your life.

Simple, right? The first time I tried this exercise, I had no clue what to write. Happiness wasn't a factor in my goal setting or my achievements. In my mind, happiness came later, after I'd achieved everything I wanted; I saw it as something to experience in hindsight, not in the moment. Still, when I sat down to complete the exercise, I was already a pretty successful guy, so I assumed I must be happy as well. What were my absolute biggest achievements? I wrote down the numbers one to five and began listing my proudest accomplishments. I put down when I won the Rookie of the Year award. I listed the first time I hit a million dollars.

Then one day, a few months later, I went swimming with my family. This was a time when I was already making small changes to the way I lived. I had stopped working 24/7 and was spending time on my marriage. I was contemplating what I actually wanted, which seemed to be an adventurous and fulfilling life with the people I loved.

That day, I was sitting in the hot tub and watching my kids play in the pool. When my kids asked me to play with them, I wasn't too enthusiastic about it, but I got my ass out of the hot tub and joined them in the water. We played. I threw them around, we splashed about, and we were having a great time. All of a sudden, a realization hit me like a freight train—I was happy. My exact thought was, *Holy shit, I'm having one of the happiest days of my life right now.* On the heels of that came the next staggering insight: *Wow, that was easy.* And then the next one hit me, and it was a real gut punch:

I can have the happiest day of my life every day.

The moment I understood this, I felt a huge shift. I realized it wasn't all that difficult to have an amazing life. I had always believed I needed an insane amount of wealth and passive income to be happy, but I didn't. The life I craved was right there, within reach.

I encourage you to actually do this exercise. Pause here, in the middle of this chapter, and write down the five happiest days of your life. Just write the numbers one to five and see what comes up. Maybe it was the time you went hiking, or kissed your wife at the top of a mountain, or took a course that challenged you. Maybe it was when you held your kid in your hands. In each of those days is a seed of what sets you on fire, what makes your years worth living. Once you have your five days, ask yourself, are you living that life right now? Because this should be in your business plan. This is where setting your compass begins.

CASE STUDY:
Meryana Discovers a New Path

Examining what we truly want can throw up all sorts of surprising answers. One of my clients, Meryana, was a very successful real estate agent. When we worked together, she had recently quadrupled her business and was on a growth trajectory. There was only one problem: through our coaching sessions, she realized she didn't want to be a real estate agent. She wasn't happy. Her calling was to write.

We designed a plan for her to exit the real estate business. Now she's moved from Edmonton, Alberta, a place that didn't make her feel alive, to Montreal, Quebec, a city that feeds her artistic core. She's about to publish a book. We talk once in a while about how fulfilled she is, far more than when she hit enormous levels of success as a real estate agent.

The Dangers of
Not Setting Your Compass

*"I think everybody should get rich and
famous and do everything they ever dreamed of
so they can see that it's not the answer."*

—Jim Carrey

There is a real danger to not setting your compass around goals that are authentic to you. If you don't get clear on what you want, other people will set your compass for you.

If I was to look you in the eye and say, *I'm going to control you*, how would you respond? Probably, you'd hit right back, saying, *Fuck no*. No one likes to be controlled. Most of us don't even like to be told what to do. Yet, that's exactly what you're agreeing to when you neglect to examine your emotions, discover what fuels you, and set your compass to those coordinates. You let people control you. You follow blindly, without pause or question. You become embroiled in a life *they* would have you live, rather than the one you want.

Let me ask you this: have you ever compared yourself to someone? Have you become lost in the comparison and grown jealous or obsessed with having what they have? This comes from not setting your compass. When you don't know what you want, it's easy to covet what others have. You might even be tempted to change direction in search of it. But when you've set your compass, you know your true north. Someone else's trajectory can't sway you.

Setting your compass also helps you define how much is enough. So many real estate agents chase sales because their financial goals are not anchored to their dreams; as soon as they reach one financial milestone, they move the goalposts. Once you link your authentic desires and your financial targets, however, you can calculate how much money you need to live a fulfilling life. When you do this, your financial targets will be based on rock-solid goals. You will no longer be pursuing growth for its own sake but for a purpose.

CASE STUDY:
How Much Is Enough?

In one of my coaching classes, I worked with a client whose real estate business was already highly successful. We were training her on world-class client experiences—helping her set up systems, training her teams, and so on. One day, she came to me and said, *There's a company that will take over my social media marketing for $6,000.*

I asked why she wanted to spend six grand on social media marketing. She told me she needed to because she was being left behind: all her competitors were crushing the social media game and she felt obsolete. I asked her how much she made per year, and we discovered it was about $400,000–$500,000. So I put a very simple question to her: was that enough money for her to live the life she wanted?

She thought about it. As part of the course, she had already set her compass, so she knew her goals. I followed up with another question: was there any place in her business where that $6,000 may be better spent? Client experience perhaps or administrative systems?

As a result of the conversation, she realizes that she didn't need social media marketing. We also discovered that she didn't even *like* it; she was doing it because she felt she had to. She was about to invest money in something that wouldn't serve her and would only intensify the pressure she was already under. The conversation helped her clarify her goals and understand that instead of pumping six grand into secur-ing sales she didn't need, she could put that money toward building out her business. Her compass helped her make a sound financial decision.

In the real estate industry, if you don't get clear on what you want, your brokerage and other agents will tell you what targets to hit, how many deals to achieve, and what financial awards you should be gunning for. If you set high goals and they are not yours, they will just create high internal pressure that will affect your performance, family, and mental health. Other people's dreams are not what you want. They are what everyone else thinks you should want. When you chase those goals for them, they're delighted.

But what do *you* want? What will light you up?

I'm definitely *not* demonizing money here. There is absolutely nothing wrong with having a million dollars, or wanting a house in LA, or dreaming of driving a Ferrari. But it has to be *your* goal, not someone else's. How ridiculous would it be to work yourself into the ground saving up for a Ferrari if you don't like cars? But if buying a Ferrari is what you want because it lights you up from the inside and because the thought of driving it fills you with so much anticipation you can't fall asleep, then owning a Ferrari is a great goal. It's your dream.

Making money is not the problem; the problem is allowing the desire to make money crush what you care about. I love that I've made a million dollars. I love that I live in one of the most beautiful places in the world and I have a bank balance that funds my lifestyle, my vacations, and all the crazy adventures I dream of creating. I absolutely live the life of the 1 percent and I'm delighted about it. But I will walk away in seconds if it affects what I want.

Also remember that, paradoxically, *not* chasing money helps you attract as much as you want. You become the guy who is magnetic versus the person who is obnoxiously about getting everything they can. Imagine meeting someone who desperately wants something from you versus the person you want to be around. Chasing doesn't help. Set your compass, focus on what matters, and the money will flow to you.

Another risk of not setting your compass is that you'll bully yourself to convince yourself to take action. I've seen real estate agents who motivate themselves using extreme methods. Clients have asked me to kick their ass to get them moving. It's a terrible strategy but a great insight into their psyche. They believe hiring a coach to yell at them is a sensible way of reaching their next milestone. Not once do they ask, *is this a milestone I want?* It's like having an elephant tell me, *Ben, you got to kick my ass so I can climb that tree. I don't care how hard it is; just berate me until I get it done.* But up a tree is clearly not where an elephant belongs. No amount of yelling will change that.

These clients have been bullying themselves for so long that they think it's the best way to motivate themselves. If you recognize yourself in this description, be careful. If you beat yourself up, you're going to attract people who beat you up, too. They won't value you because you don't value yourself.

Aggression isn't the answer, and yet so many think it is the *only* answer. But there is another way. If you love what you do, no one needs to yell at you. If you hate running, of course you need to be pushed out the door. But if you love it, you are awake half an hour early, eager to start. Your motivation is tied to what you love.

This is why setting your compass is so critical: it builds your business around what you love. Everything comes down to this: what are you built for? And how do you shape your company around what you care about so that you can wake up every single morning with 110 percent energy, raring to go? That's the ultimate competitive edge.

Energy: Your Competitive Edge

Energy determines your success, not simply knowledge. We talked about this a bit in the last chapter, but let's deep dive into it here, because setting your compass and chasing what you truly love will determine how much energy you have.

According to a poverty mindset, the trick to success is learning a new process or figuring out a secret method. But the truth is, if you're running at half energy, no secret method will save you. Energy is what makes you charismatic and magnetic; it's what makes people want to work with you and gives you the fortitude to weather the roller coaster of emotions that is an inevitable part of running a real estate business. If you're operating every day at low energy, every task will feel longer and more cumbersome. The days drag on and you fall behind.

This is why setting your compass is so important. When you're chasing what you love and not someone else's dreams, you're intrinsically motivated. You have fuel. You don't have to yell at yourself to get out of bed or hire someone to kick your ass. You have the energy to do your work because you want to. Millions of real estate agents underestimate the power of this. If your energy is high, you will crush your goals. If not, you won't succeed.

There is a difference, however, between energy and hyperactivity. Energy is an indestructible cocktail of joy, power, and eagerness. It's that feeling you get when you jump into your dream car, press the pedal, and your whole body thrums with delight. Energy flows from the bottom of your belly to the top of your spine and it gives you a deep sense of vitality.

Hyperactivity is energy at a different frequency: it is loud, brash, and scattered. I know because I have ADHD. When we think of energy, it's easy to imagine the rock star who is running across the stage, dripping sweat, screaming into the mic. But don't forget the singer sitting on a stool, quietly strumming his acoustic guitar. That's energy. It takes incredible energy to hold the attention of an audience with nothing but a guitar and a voice. But when it's done well, you could cut the atmosphere in the room with a knife.

You can't generate energy externally; it comes from within and it comes from what fuels you. We usually have low energy for two reasons: (1) we're not energizing ourselves with activities that we are passionate about, and (2) we're leaking energy by taking on a hundred tasks we hate.

Energy leaks are the death of a business. You cannot operate on 60 percent energy and win—it's not feasible. I'm from Canada and I'm an Edmonton Oilers fan (if you're an Edmonton Oilers fan, message me—you're my tribe). Connor McDavid of the Edmonton Oilers is the best hockey player in the world; I would say five times better than anyone else on the ice. Every time he's out there, he puts everyone to shame. He's whiplash fast and his skills are mind-blowing.

But what if Connor McDavid showed up to a game hungover? What if he showed up to the game not having worked out for four months? He would be terrible on the ice; he'd go from great to average, at best. It's simple practical thinking. If his energy is low, it doesn't matter how many hours he spends practicing shooting the puck or how talented he is. None of it matters if he's not energized.

The same principle applies to you. If you're leaking energy, I can coach you for decades, but you won't be able to grow your business. You will always be firefighting on another front. Imagine a fisherman trying to fish in a boat that's leaking. He spends half his time fishing and half his time trying to scoop out water from the bottom of his boat. That's not a successful fishing trip.

That's why I perform an energy audit with my clients. We explore their thinking, whom they spend time with, what activities cost them energy, and even where they live. We categorize every activity based on whether it energizes them, is neutral, or drains them. My clients have so many aha moments during these audits because they suddenly realize what has been slowly sucking the life out of them. All of a sudden, they can change it, eliminate it, or outsource it. And they win.

Here's an example of how powerful discovering and eliminating energy leaks can be, courtesy of another client. She was executing the systems I taught her—the deal flow emails, hiring an assistant, the birthday system—but she wasn't seeing results. I couldn't understand it because I knew these systems work.

She came to every coaching call with me exhausted, like she'd been sapped clean of energy. So we discussed the situation, and I learned she was having issues with her family. Her home was a space where she felt she couldn't be herself. She hated confrontation, and her previous husband had reacted aggressively during disputes. As a result, she feared discussing anything that bothered her with her new husband. Managing her reactions took an enormous amount of energy, which she couldn't pour into her company.

We spent the next few coaching sessions tackling her energy leaks. Even though her problem hasn't completely vanished, the situation has improved dramatically. And she has managed to build an incredible real estate business. She is working less and making more money. She's careful about her thinking and her environment and has become great at facing confrontation head-on because she understands that it takes less energy to deal with it than to avoid it. She knows she is in a challenging situation that can steal her energy, so she prioritizes that energy above everything else.

If you're in a situation that's draining your energy, one that you can't change immediately, I understand. Life is complicated and problems aren't always easy to solve. But there are ways to mitigate your energy leaks so that you have more vitality. Remember, you must protect your energy above all else. If you do, you will show up for your business in a way that's magnetic, and you will attract what you've been chasing. And you'll win.

Build a Life You Love

If you follow me on social media, you'll know there is one hashtag I love: #buildalifeyoulove. Instead of starting your journey with a financial goal, begin by setting your compass around what you love. When you get clear on your passions, you can build a business to serve this mission. Working toward a financial goal may generate great wealth, but if the goal is not connected to a meaningful dream or intention, you won't reach a life you love. The people I work with want more than just money: they want to truly, passionately live.

When you're working toward a goal that is authentic to you, you won't need to scream at yourself to do your work. You'll stop labeling yourself a procrastinator. You'll find the mental peace that comes from no longer living someone else's life. Listen to any talk by a successful businessman and they will tell you to do what fires you up. It's because doing what you care about gives you energy, energy makes you more attractive, and having the life you want becomes so much easier. It's the ultimate hack.

I once worked with a woman who came to every coaching call depressed. Her sales were low and she wanted me to give her a process to fix her problems. I wouldn't do it. She had an energy problem she needed to address first. But she didn't want to—she actually fought with me on the group coaching call about it. I didn't mind; I'm willing to fight someone when they're not fighting for themselves.

Three weeks into the course, with me challenging her every step of the way, she talked about how she used to train horses and compete in dressage. Six weeks in, I saw a picture of her on social media standing next to a horse with a blue ribbon. That week, she came to the call and said she made three sales.

Do not downplay the power of being you. My client struggled each day for years to make a sale, and she cracked it when she tapped into her energy source of working and competing with horses. This is what fueled her, and it gave her energy to bring to her work. She became magnetic.

It's not just her—I've seen this with hundreds of clients. There is a direct correlation between success, setting your compass, and the energy that fuels your life. Begin your journey now. Start with something small: take one step toward what you dream of. Think of my client who booked those singing lessons. One step will become two and then three. Before you know it, you will be living the life you want and those five happiest days of your life will become your everyday baseline.

What Fires Me Up

I want to end this chapter with a personal story. As a little boy, when I was still innocent, about seven years before I got lost in the street life of drugs and crime, I remember watching Wayne Gretzky and the Edmonton Oilers dominating every other side in the NHL playoffs. I wanted to play. Desperately. So I asked my parents if I could get some skates, and what do you know, they said yes.

I remember driving to that used skates shop; it felt like Christmas morning. I was so excited that it felt like my heart would leap out of my chest. I was in the back seat of the car, right behind the driver's seat, dreaming of getting those skates and what it would be like if I actually got to play hockey. Being an extrovert, I opened my mouth and said, "Man, maybe someday I could get goalie pads as well. Wouldn't that be cool?"

I'm not sure what my dad was going through at the time, but he didn't take this well. "Oh, so you want goalie pads now, too, is it?" he said. "Not happy with only skates?" And he turned the car around and drove back home. I didn't get my skates. I was devastated.

Over the years, I buried my dream of playing hockey. I'm not sure whether it was that incident alone, but I accepted it was something I didn't get to do. In my thirties, I had totally forgotten about this event, but I started to explore what I was not doing in my life that would fuel my soul. It was then that I discovered that small boy's dream of playing hockey, still sitting there years later, waiting to be realized.

Now, you have to understand that I live in a hockey city. Everyone has played hockey since they were three; even the amateurs are great. Beginners can't just pick up skates and stumble onto the ice; no one wants to play with them because they suck. But I decided I wouldn't overthink it. With no master plan, just a determination to move toward the life I wanted, I took one step toward my goal: I bought skates.

I went to a hockey store, and they fitted me with skates. I didn't care about the money; I think I spent $900 on skates when I had nowhere to play. But those ice skates made me feel like a little boy again. It was incredible; a pure act of self-love that was hard to explain. I felt like something in me had been healed, like I got my wings and nothing could stop me. I wish I could jam that feeling onto this page because then you'd know instantly how alight your passions make you feel. You wouldn't need coffee, energy drinks, or any other external substance to lift your energy, that's for sure.

I posted a picture of those skates on social media as a way of saying to the universe, *I'm going to do what I love.* The universe answered. A real estate agent I'd known for years messaged to tell me about a league created specifically for guys like me: adult beginners, who always wanted to play hockey but never learned. I went along, and it was incredible. They taught me the basics, like how to hold the stick and lace up the gear, organized eight practices, and then set me and others like me up with four actual games. It felt like a miracle. Finally, I was playing hockey.

Fast forward a few years, and I play hockey twice a week. I've fulfilled my dream of being a general manager—granted, I don't own the Edmonton Oilers, but running the Puck Whisperers is almost as good. I named the team, built it, and led it. We've won multiple championships. I've sat in the locker room drinking beer out of a championship cup. It might not have been the Stanley Cup, but it was the beer league cup, and man, *it made me happy*.

Today, hockey is one of the non-negotiables in my life. It's the greatest energy source I have, and it helps me show up to my business every single day and build it to greater heights. More importantly, it is part of the life I dream of living—except that dream is not in some distant future but happening right now, every week.

Set your compass. Find what you love and build your business around it. Live today.

3

Your Relationship
with Fear

In 2006, I started a real estate investment company called Cashflow Consultants Ltd. We grew rapidly year on year and quickly developed a portfolio of sixty-one properties, more than twenty investors, and millions of dollars in real estate holdings. We did flips, holds, got involved in condo conversions, and had a massive vision of where we wanted to take the company. By 2008, we were poised to grow exponentially.

Then, out of nowhere, the great financial crash hit. Markets collapsed. Many thousands of people lost their livelihoods and lifetime savings. It was a scary time. My investors called me, panicked: they wanted to sell their real estate investments immediately because they'd lost everything in the stock market.

I'll be honest with you: I was young and dedicated, but I was inexperienced and had never handled this type of adversity. I wasn't used to clients calling me in a panic, relying on me to save them from financial disaster. As a people pleaser, I succeeded by working hard and clocking extra hours to give my investors good returns. But I couldn't solve this problem by working harder or boosting my performance. The world I knew was crashing, completely collapsing, and I had no reference point to cling to, nothing to hold on to.

It was a dark time in my life. Looking back on it now, I could reel off a list of people who went through similar trials. Businessmen, investors, financial planners—everyone was watching what they knew crumble and navigating a new, painful reality. Everyone was lost. At the time, however, I felt like I was the only one. It was an incredibly lonely sensation. I didn't know whom to speak to or how to work my way out of the challenges I was facing. As more investors called to pull their money out, I had to tell them I didn't have a solution for them. Letting people down was a devastating experience, and I felt the pressure build and build until I was overwhelmed.

Late one night, as I sat at the desk in my office, the full force of the situation hit me. My entire life, I'd never felt so alone. Out of sheer desperation, I put my head on my desk and cried. It was hopeless. There was no way out.

I can't explain what happened next. I don't know what you believe—

I don't even know what *I* believe—but I experienced a vision. Maybe it was God or maybe it was my subconscious; I don't know.

All I know is that suddenly I was in the ocean. Not near the surface, where the light still penetrated, but in the depths. Everything around me was dark. Slowly, inexorably, I was sinking, as though I had weights strapped to my ankles. As I sunk deeper and deeper, fear gripped me. I panicked. My breath grew erratic, my heart constricted, and my mind screamed at me to swim, to fight, to get to the surface. I kept sinking. The water pressure was crushing, all traces of light disappearing as it got darker. I lost all vision. In the dark, I couldn't see a thing and had the feeling that I was going to die.

But then I heard another voice, saying, *keep going.*

Every cell in my body was screaming at me to turn back. My mind told me I was going to die. But the small voice inside me said, *keep going. The seabed is where all the sunken ships are. That's where the gold is.*

I kept going. Despite the fear, I trusted that small voice and leaned into the darkness and mounting pressure. And the voice was right: as I felt around in the dark, I started to find gold. The seabed was covered with rotting ships, their hulls split open, treasure spilling out.

When I awoke, I listened to the voice. I leaned into the darkness and the feelings I didn't want to face. I moved toward my fear, not away from it. I kept going. I told myself I would never be here again so I must take advantage of this situation. If I didn't, I would miss out on what it could teach me. The 2008 crash was one of the most difficult business scenarios I navigated, but I can tell you now I did find the gold. I know what it's like to come back and rebuild. I know what it is like to be lost, unable to see a way forward and feel incredible pressure from every side. I know how powerful and important it is to feel those negative emotions, examine them, and get to know them. If you're in a bad place and think you're alone, you're not. Keep swimming to the sunken ships so you can get the treasure. Remember, you're never going to be here again.

Fear Is Your Friend

If fear was a person, what would you say to them? Would you greet them as a friend or push them away as an enemy?

I'm constantly hearing people talk about defeating their fear. "Fight your fear!" "Feel no fear!" "Ten ways to overcome your fear!" For thousands of years, we've demonized and battled this feeling. And for thousands of years, we've lost.

When people tell me they will fight their fears, it always makes me laugh. Fear has been around for centuries, participating in millions of these "fights" with humankind. Fear has won every time. If it hadn't, it wouldn't be around. Do you think you will be the first person to defeat fear?

This loss is inevitable because we aren't meant to battle our fear. Fear is an emotion. Imagine replacing the word "fear" with "laughter" in the sayings above. It would sound ridiculous. "Fight your laughter!" "Feel no laughter!" "Ten ways to overcome your laughter!" Would you fight your laughter? If your answer is, *of course not, that's silly*, then why are you fighting your fear?

Fear is our advisor. It keeps us safe every day, warning us about the many ways we can come to harm. Even though I didn't listen to it during my vision, my fear was right. It told me to turn back because, based on historical data, it thought I would drown. It was the logical conclusion. Fear wasn't trying to sabotage me or keep me from the gold at the bottom of the sea. It wanted to save me.

We don't need to demonize fear. We need to befriend it.

As part of my coaching course, I've asked thousands of real estate agents what their lives and businesses would look like if fear wasn't holding them back. These are some of their answers, taken straight from the surveys:

- I would be kicking in doors, getting listing appointments.

- I would most likely be running a real estate team.

- I would be a millionaire many times over.

- I would explode. I believe my business would grow in leaps and bounds.

- I would remove obstacles in my head.

- I would finally hire an assistant and get a buyer's agent.

- I would be substantial and growing.

This is why most coaching doesn't work: we're trying to solve emotional problems with a practical solution. These statements demonstrate how brilliant agents believe their lives could be if they weren't held back by fear, and yet *no one* in real estate coaching is actually addressing fear. Instead, coaches encourage clients to work on lead generation, or building a team, or changing brokerages. It's like having a broken leg and putting the sling on your arm—it won't heal you. We look outward for a solution when we should be looking inward.

When we look inward, the potential for growth is exponential. Sure, learning better lead generation skills may increase your business by 10 or 15 percent, but it's a small change that takes a lot of effort and likely won't last. Working on your mindset, your emotions, your inner game—that's the secret to growing *10x*. The real hack to leveling up your business is understanding your emotions.

When I talk about understanding emotions, I mean we must form relationships with them. I've coached clients who spent countless hours trying to outrun or outthink their fear. It doesn't work. When they focus on understanding their fear, however, and making friends with it, they develop their inner game. I've seen people double and triple their income purely by nurturing this relationship.

The same approach can work for you.

Understanding Your Fear

To form a genuine relationship with fear, you must first understand what it is.

Fear works in tandem with our brain. Our brain understands the world using historical data, collected over a lifetime of past experiences. Based on the data it receives, it interprets the future so we can navigate our surroundings more effectively. In other words, your brain predicts your future based on historical data.

Fear is the emotion your brain conjures to keep you safe and maintain control in the confusing, chaotic world in which we exist. If you slip on ice once, your brain will make a mental note that ice is slippery. Then, because it doesn't want you to slip again, it conjures fear, which shows up faithfully to say, *Be careful of the ice. If you walk on it, bad things will happen.*

Fear isn't wrong. It is advising you based on what it knows. Ice *is* slippery and you *did* slip on it and injure yourself. According to fear, it makes sense that you should never venture onto the ice again because every time you do, you'll hurt yourself.

Let's explore a more extreme example. Imagine a child who has heard noises in the night and decided there is a monster in the closet. Maybe he read a book featuring monsters. Maybe he heard from other kids in the neighborhood that monsters live in closets. Either way, the brain has what it considers reliable data that there is a monster in the closet, and now the child is petrified.

In this situation, fear appears to keep the child safe. If there really *is* a monster in the closet, confronting the monster will result in certain death. So fear keeps the child in bed, under the covers. It tells the child, *Don't move or the monster will get us.* The kid's heart is galloping; he is anxious and trembling. It is the worst night of his life.

The solution isn't to yell at fear and fight it. The solution is to provide new data. The child must turn on the light, walk up to the closet, and throw open the doors. He needs to show fear that there is no monster. Once fear learns this, it can offer the kid better information. The next time fear thinks there are monsters in his closet, the brain can respond, *You might feel like there is a monster, but we checked and there definitely isn't. Don't worry. You can sleep easy.*

But if the kid doesn't educate his fear, he will stay in bed night after night, petrified, because fear will tell him a monster wants to kill him; it doesn't know any better.

Shouting at your fear isn't the answer. Fear is a loyal friend; it always protects you, irrespective of how often you tell it to fuck off. Fear is *useful*. Imagine, for a second, what our world would look like if we weren't afraid. It would be absolute anarchy. People wouldn't wear harnesses to climb mountains. They'd cross the road without looking. They'd put their hands into fires. They'd throw themselves into the path of danger, again and again, because there would be no advisor to pipe up and say, *maybe this is a bad idea.*

I always imagine fear as a sober friend at a party. You've gone out drinking, had an amazing night, and now it's time to go home. You're wasted but convinced you can drive. Fear is the friend telling you you can't drive. They take your car keys and hide them. You're drunk and furious with them, but the next morning, you are very grateful they were there.

If we want to harness the power of our fear, we must partner with it. We have to stop seeing it as the enemy. Remember, fear is always advising you based on past experiences. For example, one of the most common fears on the planet is public speaking. Most people are petrified of public speaking, whether they've tried it or not. Why? Because the moment they think about giving a speech, fear calls up memories of times they were laughed at, or humiliated, or when they made a fool of themselves. It reminds them of the pain of being judged and then advises them to avoid it, like any friend would.

But just because fear has our best interests at heart, it doesn't mean we should always listen to it. Question your fear. Discover whether it is advising you based on old or inaccurate data. If it is, move past that advice, like the child who threw open his closet to discover the monster was imaginary.

It's critical to understand that we are not our fears. Demonizing fear robs us of the opportunity to learn from it. Stay in the moment and learn what you can. Grow. Just like me in my vision, you might be sinking into the depths of the black ocean, but you're closing in on the gold. If you swim toward the surface now, you'll miss the opportunity to grab the treasure.

I know this is difficult to do. When you're scared, you don't want to prolong the feeling; you want it to end. But I promise, these dark and pressurized moments are incredible fuel for learning. You learn far more when you're scared than when you're feeling powerful and confident, because fear opens you up to receive the lessons the situation is offering you. Harness that. The next time you feel afraid, don't run for the hills. Keep going. Build a relationship with fear. Make it your partner.

Building a Relationship with Fear

I know it sounds abstract to say "Build a relationship with fear," so let's break this concept down into practical terms. Forging a relationship with fear is all about building a relationship with yourself.

As you know by now, fear isn't your enemy. It's an emotion that comes *from* you. Every time you fight it or despise it, you are fighting yourself. Every time you say *Get out of here, fear!* you're giving yourself the same message. This is a powerful lesson, because we are so good at disparaging fear and viewing it as separate from ourselves. But it isn't. No wonder the world struggles with anxiety and depression: how are we meant to find self-love if we can't love fear, which is a part of ourselves? It's like saying you adore everything about yourself, except for your left foot. Burying your fear, battling with it, berating it—these are unhealthy ways to tackle what scares you.

This applies to trust as well. If you don't trust your fear, you don't entirely trust yourself. This mistrust percolates into your business partnerships, your friendships, and your family relationships. It corrodes and corrupts.

Forming authentic relationships with ourselves is not easy. Society has normalized burying our negative emotions to the point where we never examine them. In real estate coaching, I encounter this tendency all the time. One of the tools I use in my sessions is exploring negative reactions: asking ourselves why we react to something is a beautiful doorway into personal insight and growth, not to mention the development of our emotional intelligence. But many people don't want to examine their negative reactions. They want to feel good all the time and so when they feel bad, they run from it.

It is equally unhealthy to pretend that your fear has nothing to do with you. Have you heard the phrase "The devil made me do it"? It's a cop-out, an easy way to abdicate responsibility. People use their fear in the same manner. It becomes this demon that is holding them back so that they themselves don't have to change. They remain victims forever.

Here is the hard truth: fear cannot steal anything from you. Anything you believe fear has taken from you, you have given away freely. Year after year, I hand out my surveys in my coaching classes, and each year, clients tell me what they would do if fear wasn't holding them back. But fear isn't. They are restricting themselves. Why aren't we partnering with fear to move forward together?

Become the Witness, Not the Judge

The first step to befriending your fear is to become a witness, not a judge. What do I mean by this? Picture a scene in a courtroom, complete with lawyers, a judge, and a witness on the stand. What is the job of this witness? They are called on to testify, which means they state what they saw. They aren't allowed to have an opinion about what they saw. If they try to provide one, a lawyer immediately objects and their opinion is struck from the record. The role of a witness is only to observe and report.

Now think about the judge, sitting there with his wig and gavel. His role is to pass judgment. The moment he reaches that judgment and bangs that gavel down, the case is closed. We do the same with fear. As soon as it emerges to deliver a testimony, we rush prematurely to judgment. If we can slow down and instead become the witness, we can discover what fear has to tell us and only *then* determine whether it offers wise counsel.

Strive to be a witness in your relationship to fear. Observe what you're feeling and why, but do not judge it. This is harder than it sounds. All of us critique ourselves; in our heads, we're our harshest bullies. Even that nice old Christian lady is worried about whether she is nice enough or Christian enough. But true emotional intelligence comes from observing our feelings without self-judgment. Because the moment we judge, we close the case. We are no longer listening to what fear has to teach us; we've already decided what fear means. After that, nothing can help us.

Forming an authentic relationship with yourself depends on you becoming the witness to your emotions, not the judge. When you do this, you create the space to befriend your fear. Until then, you'll dismiss what it has to teach you. And the longer you ignore those lessons, the easier it is for this state of deafness to become your new normal until you forget how good life could be. It's like sleep. If you haven't slept for days and then pass out for four hours, you feel fantastic. But the reality is, four hours is much less than the eight hours you need.

What Happens When We Ignore Fear?

Imagine this scenario. A man goes out surfing, has an accident, and breaks his leg. He knows he should go to the doctor, but he doesn't like hospitals or the clinic, so he doesn't go. Instead, he watches a few YouTube videos on how to heal a broken leg and makes his own splint. It hurts for weeks, but he pushes through the pain.

Eventually, the leg seems to heal, but it sets wrong. He walks with a limp. He can drive and get groceries, but he can't do things he used to love, like climbing mountains or running races. For a while, he continues with this new normal. When it gets too much, though, he looks fear in the eye and decides he can't live at half-capacity anymore. He's going to a doctor.

The doctor takes a look and says, sure, he can fix the man's limp. But because the man waited so long, the bone has fully healed in a crooked position. The only way forward is to break the man's leg again and reset it properly.

The man hesitates. The pain was bad the first time; does he really want to endure a broken leg again? But he thinks about everything he's missing out on in life, and he agrees. This time, the pain is much worse. But after six to eight weeks, the leg heals completely and the man's limp is gone. He can go mountaineering and enter marathons again. He's living the life he wants to live.

If he hadn't waited so long to confront fear, he could have saved himself a lot of unnecessary pain. But on the other hand, if he hadn't finally embraced the pain or leaned into the fear, he couldn't have reached his full potential. He needed a fully functioning leg to chase his passions—no amount of extra training or rock-climbing lessons would have offset that limp.

It's exactly the same with our emotions. We can avoid our emotions and make it through life at half-capacity. It's possible. You can function on four hours of sleep. That man could walk with a limp. But I promise you, you won't reach your full potential or experience life to its fullest. Who wants that?

Move Forward with Your Fear

My aim in this chapter is not only to teach you how to reframe the concept of fear but also to give you practical tools you can use as a real estate agent.

You already know that fear is your friend and advisor and also that it sometimes gives you poor advice because it doesn't have up-to-date data. You understand that to partner effectively with fear, you need to educate it. You also know that you won't succeed by judging your emotions. In order to learn from what fear is teaching you, you need to observe and listen as a witness would.

But how do you translate these learnings into actionable advice? Here is a simple but powerful place to start: Keep moving forward.

So many of us get stuck thinking about what we don't know or can't handle. We try to learn as much as we can, spending all our time in the preparation phase. Don't fall into this trap. Move forward. Act. If you are someone who needs to know everything before taking action, you're probably just using incomplete information as a way to avoid fear.

You can't learn your way to success, especially not in real estate. Think about it: if you miraculously got three listings this week, don't you think you would figure out how to handle them, whether or not you felt ready? You are always a faster and more effective learner when you *get* a client and work with them. This is where phrases like "fail forward" come from. They reflect the fact that in order to progress, we have to keep moving.

Moving forward is also how you educate your fear. If you're petrified of getting a client because you think you will mess up, the only way to educate your fear is to get one. Think of the boy who believed he had a monster in his closet. He educated his fear by opening the cupboard and showing his fear there was no monster. He had to keep moving forward, no matter how much he wanted to stay in bed under the covers.

When I first started a podcast, I had no clue what I was doing. I didn't know how to record or edit or frame episodes. I decided I didn't care how bad it was at first; I wanted to do it. So I bought a mic, found a guy who could set up the backend for $700, and started. All I needed to get going was a few guests, and I made it work. I kept moving forward.

Today, I have recorded more than a hundred episodes. Each one is informed by the mistakes I have made along the way. I needed to fail, repeatedly, to provide my fear with new data and learn how to create an amazing podcast. Once my fear had the new data, it could give me better advice the next time I encountered a challenge. This is how you succeed: one step at a time.

Netflix has a similar story. When the company first launched, they were obsessed with cosmopolitan details such as website design, layout, and presentation. They tried out different business ideas, taking ages to launch each one. As idea after idea bombed, however, they realized they would never succeed by taking so long to launch each one. If they wanted to be at the forefront of innovation, they couldn't waste time obsessing about the small things. They needed to speed up how often they "failed" so they could learn from their mistakes. So they set a different rhythm: they launched new ideas quickly, with basic—even sloppy—websites. Launch, test, fail, repeat: this was their pattern.

Today, they're Netflix. No one thinks to themselves *I wish Netflix spent more time on the color scheme of those initial websites.* No one cares, because Netflix learned from the mistakes that mattered and built an incredibly successful company. Today, they are entertainment giants.

Many of my clients want to mitigate their fear and their risk before they move forward. But this attitude will slow you down. It will keep you stuck, pressed against a glass ceiling of your own making. Just take a step forward. Often, that's the only way to learn how to navigate the next step and then the next.

Fear in the Real World

Not working with your fear can have genuine consequences in the real world. Fear can cost you millions of dollars in your business, while educating it can free you to pursue your dreams.

Here's a powerful parable about how fear and insecurity can hold you back. Imagine a real estate agent doing a listing presentation with a potential seller. She has spent hours preparing for this meeting. Yet, she gets into a rush on the day of the pitch and runs out of time to apply her makeup.

This woman is beautiful, both externally and internally. But she's used to always wearing makeup, and she feels naked without it. Instantly, she becomes insecure. Fear tells her that the sellers are laughing at her because she looks unprofessional and ridiculous. Feeling self-conscious, she wants to go home and apply makeup, but she doesn't have time.

She buries her fear and focuses on her presentation. Objectively, the presentation is great. She has prepared meticulously and is the right person for the job. But her lack of makeup plays on her mind. She tries to hide the insecurity she feels from her potential clients, but the act of hiding gets in her head and affects her behavior. She doesn't come across strongly; she repeatedly touches her face, wondering whether the seller is noticing her lack of makeup. The sellers can tell she's hiding something—and they're right! She's hiding her fears about how she looks. But all they know is that something feels off. She comes across as untrustworthy. In the end, the sellers go with someone else, thinking there's just "something about her" that doesn't feel right.

Vulnerability is always better displayed than hidden. How could she have handled the situation differently? She could have owned up to her insecurity. She could have said, *You know what? I was so excited about listing your home that I ran out of time to put on makeup today. How crazy is that?* She could have laughed about it with them and broken down the barriers of mistrust.

If you can accept your shortcomings and love yourself, you can let people see you clearly. I know this sounds terrifying, but trust me, people will appreciate you for it. You will become magnetic, you will land more listings, and people will refer you. This is the power of harnessing your emotional intelligence and forming a relationship with your fear.

Remember, fear's advice isn't constant. It can change if you educate it. I once coached a real estate agent whose business was amazing. She was incredibly successful, and I kept wondering why she wouldn't hire staff to help her. All she wanted was some time off and to recharge, but she had no one to share the workload. When I suggested she get an assistant, she was reluctant. It turned out she had hired once before and it didn't work out.

Fear told her that every assistant would be like the first, costing her money and time. She needed to educate it so it could give her better advice, but the only way to do that was to hire again.

It took some time for me to convince her that hiring the right person would be a game changer. When she finally hired again, it turned out I was right: the person was spectacular. Her business took off, and she was free to spend summers at the lake and reconnect with her family. The *story* changed. From believing that every hire is awful, she now praises the benefits of having a team.

It's a lot like door knocking. I've spoken to hundreds of people who refused to door knock because they were petrified of rejection. No one wants to get doors slammed in their face or be yelled at by strangers. But many people are actually very welcoming or at least friendly. Sure, you'll get the occasional person who is impatient or having a bad day, but mostly you'll meet people who are happy you stopped by and are interested in hearing what you have to say. But to learn this, you have to do the thing you're scared of doing. You have to knock on doors.

Indeed, the overall narrative around door knocking is now changing. No one does it anymore, not since the internet arrived, which means door knocking is now special. You're not interrupting someone's day to sell them something; you're connecting with them and getting to know them better. You're tapping into a nostalgic time when people used to stop by houses to communicate and connect.

The key is to give fear new data so it can change the story. When I coach real estate agents, they tell me they want to be the go-to guy in the area. This is the number one aspirational goal for an agent: to be the person everyone in the area thinks of when it comes to buying and selling properties. Of course, you can't be the go-to guy if no one knows you exist, so the first step is to be more visible. But the moment I ask my clients to do a Facebook Live or an Instagram Live, they clam up. They don't want to. Fear tells them they will be judged.

In our coaching sessions, we change this narrative. I insist that they hop onto a Facebook Live so they can see it's not threatening. Are people annoyed to see them pop up on their feed? Not at all. Most of the comments are about how lovely it is to hear from them and learn about what they're doing. People care. The moment my coaching clients realize this, they reeducate their fear. They know there is a chance of being laughed at, but there's a greater chance they will make meaningful connections and find good business.

I want to leave you with one last story, because educating your fear is truly one of the most powerful things you can do for your business and I want you to grasp its real-world implications. I was coaching an agent called Mariana who needed to call some of her old clients. I remember we were in a face-to-face meeting as she explained why she couldn't call them. She hadn't talked to them for two years. They would be mad at her for not keeping in touch. If she called after such a long time, they would think she was usurious, only calling when she wanted business. She absolutely could not pick up that phone.

The loop of anxiety and fear she'd spun for herself was intense. She was agonized about calling these clients. So I provided her fear with new information. I opened a drawer in my desk and pulled out a contact book. Do you know those old books where you store people's contact cards, a bit like a photo album? I opened one of those. I chose the contact of a developer I'd worked with seven years back. His name was Brad. I hadn't spoken to him since then.

I began to dial.

As I waited for him to pick up, I told Mariana that there was no point guessing what clients she hadn't spoken to in two years would think. I was calling someone I hadn't spoken to in *seven* years. Let's see how it went.

As you can guess, it went great. Miraculously, Brad had kept his old phone number and he was delighted to hear from me. We swapped updates for two or three minutes. At the end of the call, he asked if I could check out a property for him that he was looking to sell. I said it was no problem.

Fear was simply giving Mariana bad advice. Old clients do want to hear from you and no one blames you for being busy. I proved that her worries were based on faulty data, she educated her fear, and she moved on. Now, if Mariana needs to call old clients, she just picks up the phone. She's experienced real practical benefits from creating a relationship with her fear and moving forward anyway.

Face Your Garden Snake

In many ways, what we've discussed in this chapter comes down to emotional intelligence. To succeed in life and in the real estate business, you must be intelligent about your emotions. If you want to keep your clients for life and have them refer you for twenty years or more, then you must form a connection with them. But creating a deep connection with other people is impossible unless you have a deep connection with yourself, which means partnering with your fear.

This is more important than the practical skills that go into being a real estate agent. It's a hundred times more impactful than honing your lead generation skills. As we saw in Chapter 1, most people are trying to solve emotional problems with practical business solutions, which doesn't work. If you focus on developing your emotional intelligence and making friends with your fear, you'll address the real issues. Once you do, there's no limit to what you can achieve.

This change is not temporary; it's not a flash-in-the-pan solution. Once you understand your relationship with fear, you will permanently alter how you live your life.

Imagine a house that is beautifully kept, but the yard is overflowing with weeds. The fence hasn't been replaced in years and the paint is starting to chip away from the wood. The woman who lives in the house won't venture into this backyard because years ago, she saw a snake there.

Now, this woman is terrified of snakes. She doesn't know how this one got into her backyard, but she saw it right by the fence, viper green and curled up. She fled into the house and she hasn't been into her backyard since. She's let the weeds grow waist-high. She has ignored the fence. She won't take her friends out back, even when the weather is lovely. Her neighbors think she's a little crazy, letting her yard go like that, but she doesn't care. She never *ever* wants to risk seeing that snake again.

Then, one day, she decides enough is enough. It's *her* backyard, after all. She's going to do something about the snake. She grabs a rake and marches outside. She stops. The weeds are so high now that she can't see anything. The snake might be anywhere, lying in wait. But she takes a deep breath, holds the rake out in front of her, and walks toward where she saw it last, right by the corner of the fence.

It's still there. She can see flashes of that viper green among the weeds. Everything in her screams, *Run!* but she doesn't. She takes two steps forward and then another one. Then she starts to laugh and cries with relief.

It isn't a snake. It's a watering hose.

She's wasted years not making memories in this backyard because she was scared of something that didn't exist. She could have been gardening, lying out in the sun, and sharing barbecues with friends. But the good news is, now she's seen the truth and she can't *unsee* it. She knows the snake is actually a watering hose. She can't ever be scared of it again.

Today, fear and I are partners. Fear talks to me and I take what it says into consideration. But before I decide to listen to fear, I ask myself, Is this an old story? Or is fear advising me based on updated data?

At the end of the day, fear isn't our only advisor. It's just one of the team members. Befriend it and care for it, but evaluate what it is saying. If you find its advice is behind the curve, educate it. Like any good team member, it will catch up in no time.

Above all, follow your heart. Remember, no matter how crazy it seems, there's sunken treasure at the bottom of that sea.

I Love You, Fear

I know how challenging it is to befriend fear because I've been there. But I also know how rewarding it can be when you get the relationship right.

A few years ago, I was on a cross-Canada speaking tour. As part of the tour, I was running a two-day event in Edmonton, Alberta called "How to Blow Your Client's Minds and Keep Them For Life." It was going great. On day two, as I drove to the venue, I realized I wanted to share a poem I had written about fear.

At that time, I'd spent a few years working on my relationship with fear and I was proud of how much I'd grown. I truly cherished fear, and I loved that I could greet it as a friend. The moment I thought of sharing this poem with my audience, however, fear spoke up loudly. It reminded me of how I was the geek in school, always derided and bullied. It brought up the time I shared something vulnerable with my father and he laughed at me. It pointed out that this was a real estate event, not therapy or an art class. *Don't do it*, fear said. It didn't want to see me suffer.

When I reached the venue and climbed onto the stage, I was still warring with myself. I wanted to read this poem, but fear reminded me of all the times sharing myself vulnerably had gone terribly wrong. It showed me how awful it was to be judged. It worked to an extent: I was scared.

But I leaned into the fear. There were about a hundred people in the room and I told them about the poem and how I feared being laughed at. I told them I didn't care, though, and that I was going to read it anyway. My knees were trembling. How ridiculous is that? I had a YouTube Channel, a podcast, and had spoken across Canada in many live events, but I was still nervous.

Yet, I was also excited. Sure, fear was still telling me to not do it, but some part of me knew that if I did, it would be an incredible experience. Even if they laughed at me—and I believed they wouldn't—I would get an opportunity to level up my internal strength. I would grow.

I read the poem. Not a single person laughed. Instead, people were so touched that they cried. It was one of the most amazing and powerful moments in my life. I shared who I was with strangers, and they got to see me and accept me exactly as I am. I was *seen*. I can't explain how empowering that is.

All I had to do was lean into the fear.

I Love You, Fear

I close my eyes and see possibility,

I open my eyes and see the work that needs to be done.

I use my head to build the strategy,

but my heart holds the keys to the compass.

I continue to move forward even though

fear screams in my ear to stop.

The voice of fear is loud, but I still consider him an old friend,

a beautiful companion to keep me safe on my journey.

Fear is important to me but does not navigate anymore.

Fear keeps me safe and keeps me humble.

Thank you, fear ... thank you, my old friend.

Stop fighting fear, stop making your old friend mad, he is
here to help you.

Fear is not designed to drive your life,

fear keeps you safe, keeps you sharp

and keeps you humble.

I run forward as fast as I can when fear screams at me to hide.

Fear is the compass my heart holds the keys to.

Fear gets scared when you get close to your purpose, your passion, your freedom.

Thank you, fear, for being with me, thank you, fear, for loving me so much you would speak to me and try to help me on my journey.

You're welcome to stay with me forever,

I will always hear you out, but please remember,

the heart is the captain of this ship.

I Love You, Fear.

4

Hustler versus
Business Owner

I was at an office party, hosted by Gunnar Office Furnishings, with my wife. It was New Year's Eve. I remember the party was 1970s themed, with go-go dancers, and we were both dressed up. I don't remember much else because I wasn't really present. The whole evening, all I could think about was the property I had recently bought.

Although I still worked for Gunnar, I was starting to branch out as a real estate investor. The property I had secured, my third, was missing a tenant. Finding that tenant seemed crucial—urgent, even—but the property was a four-and-a-half-hour drive from our home. Not a short distance. But I'd scheduled a viewing for early the following morning, and I was adamant I would get there.

When the clock struck midnight, I kissed my wife and we wished everyone a happy new year. Then she headed to her car and I headed to mine so I could drive through the night and reach the property in the morning.

Looking back, I'm a little embarrassed to admit that I did this. I drove all night and spent the first day of a new year away from my family, for *one* viewing. I didn't think about my wife, waking up our kids in the morning alone. I didn't think about the time I was wasting, which I could have spent with my family. I was so proud of how hard I worked that none of this even occurred to me. Nor was this a one-off; I did things like this all the time.

The next morning, the client didn't show. I'd just driven four and a half hours one way, and was looking at another four and a half hours back, for a canceled meeting. I wish I could say I was crushed and that the experience became a wake-up call. But honestly, I wasn't even disappointed. I didn't regret driving through the night. I just got in my car, put on a CD about how to make money and be successful, and drove back home. I was obsessed.

At that time in my life, I had the mindset of a hustler. My sense of emotional lack drove me to fill a gap I didn't know existed. I was determined to prove I was worth something—that I could work harder than anyone else, push harder than anyone else. And I was willing to sacrifice anything to prove it.

Today, I look back on that guy and think he was so lost and disconnected from what matters in life. I could have just done what I would do in that situation now: call someone in the area, pay them $20, have them open the door for the client, and then talk to the client on the phone. Simple, efficient, intelligent. I do this for a whole portfolio of properties and it works like clockwork. But I fell for the myth that hard work and toil are the only route to success. It's a lie. Hard work and hustle may be how you *start* something successful, but it's not how you grow from there.

To do that, you must become a business owner.

Change Your Mindset

I magine this scenario. Your friend comes to you with wonderful news: he's just bought a restaurant. It's in a fantastic location, it has a loyal customer base, and he bought it at a bargain price because the previous owner was retiring. You're elated for him.

Then he starts describing his vision for this restaurant.

He's got it all planned out. He's going to be the cook. He's going to be the maître d'. He's going to design the new logo, select the menu, build the website, plan the marketing, wash the dishes, shovel the snow, and sweep the parking lot. It's a perfect solution, he tells you.

Much cheaper than hiring and much easier than training staff. Far less hassle than dealing with people who might make mistakes and cost him money. He's going to do it all.

At this point, you'd be looking at your friend like he was crazy. To any sane person, the imminent failure of his plan would be glaringly obvious. Hell, he would probably fail *so* fast that he would make headlines: *New owner wrecks beloved restaurant in record time.*

But this is exactly how I see real estate agents thinking. When agents come to me, they're always so *proud* of how much they do. They show properties, plan their marketing, build their websites, design their business cards, do all the listings and stagings, network at five different events, participate in BNI groups…You're probably reading this right now and thinking, *oh shit, that's me.*

Real estate agents are constantly doing four or five jobs at the same time, trying to pack as much as possible into the twenty-four hours of their day, because they think this is how to succeed. That's the mindset of a hustler. They glorify hard work, even if it leads to burnout. Like your friend who just bought a restaurant in the example above, they believe they have to do everything themselves. And because they have only twenty-four hours in a day, they're always asking, *how can I find the time to get this done?*

To achieve long-term success, you need to think differently. You need to swap that hustler mindset for the mindset of a business owner. A business owner knows he has *more* than twenty-four hours in a day to achieve what he wants because he can *hire*. He can buy someone else's time. He will never try to be the chef, maître d', marketer, and dishwasher at his restaurant because he can hire people qualified to do those jobs so that the restaurant succeeds. He always asks himself, *whose time can I buy?*

The value and impact of this distinction are huge. So many agents come to me demoralized by their business; they think they're inefficient and label themselves procrastinators. But they're not procrastinating: they're trying to do five jobs at once. No one can succeed trying to do five jobs simultaneously—it's impossible.

But they believe their struggles are their fault and their confidence takes a hit. That's the cost of a hustler mentality. According to industry wisdom, hustling gets you more sales, and sales always make you feel like you're moving forward. But *how far* are you progressing? And can you sustain it? Look at the bigger picture. Do you think your friend can do all those jobs at his restaurant and succeed? And if not, why would you follow the same business model?

One Man Can't Defeat an Army

Let's do a quick comparison of what's possible with a worker mindset versus a business owner mindset.

At every new coaching session, I like to ask my clients a question to gauge their mentality: *How many deals have you lost from a simple lack of follow-up?* As you know, poor follow-up is a common problem in our industry. You do a CMA and the sellers ask you to get in touch in three weeks, but you get busy and forget. When the For Sale sign goes up on the property, it doesn't have your name on it. Forgetting to make one phone call cost you a lucrative deal, along with the time and effort you spent putting together the presentation, pitching to those clients, and building a good impression.

Most agents say a lack of follow-up costs them about ten to twenty deals a year. Let's take ten deals as a conservative number. Let's assume each deal is worth about $10,000. I know this figure isn't standard—my friends in lower commission states need four to five deals to make that much money, whereas agents in New York or Toronto are looking at much more per deal. But let's use $10,000 as a ballpark figure and to make the math easier.

If you lose ten sales, each worth $10,000, that's $100,000 of revenue you're missing out on per year. That's a lot of money—all because you forgot to make a few phone calls.

How would a hustler handle this problem? They'd think to themselves, *I can fix this. All I have to do is get a system in place. Set reminders on my phone. Make sure I prioritize this call. It's a simple task—I know I can get it done.* But systems aren't enough to get you through that last mile. I have a "system" where I'm meant to wash my dishes the moment I finish eating. Great plan, right? Guess how often I implement it. If you think you can take responsibility for understanding why you don't make follow-up calls, create a system that bypasses your resistance, and *then* find the minutes in the day to actually make those calls, on top of your hundred other tasks, well, that type of thinking is the problem.

Here's how you switch up your mindset and approach this issue like a business owner. Instead of asking *how* to fix this, all you have to do is ask yourself, *who* can fix this? It's really that simple. Hire someone to remind you to make those follow-up calls.

Most agents won't hire because they think they don't have the money. That's bullshit. Let's break down the cost, right now, so you can dismiss this excuse once and for all. Let's say you hire someone for one hour a day to keep your list organized and to ensure you follow up with clients. You pay that person $20 an hour. Not including any unpaid vacation time, this works out at $100 a week, or $5,200 per year.

Five thousand two hundred dollars to earn a *hundred* thousand dollars. That's an incredible return on investment. Forecast this for the next ten years, and you end up paying this person $52,000 *maximum*—to earn $1 million.

This is why a hustler can never compete with a business owner: they're only one man versus the business owner's army. They don't have the advantage of time. A worker has twenty-four hours in a day. Factor in time for essentials such as eating and sleeping, and that goes down to fifteen hours, maximum. But a business owner can hire five full-time employees to make the most of his time. That's five times more work, profit, and growth.

Shifting my mindset from worker to business owner changed my life. When I outsourced what drained me and focused on what I was good at, everything became easier. It blows my mind that I can spend the same amount of money as I spend on lunch to buy an hour of someone's time. Why would you not do it? Why would you not pay someone to help you streamline your life so you can focus on what you care about?

I'll be honest: buying time does feel like I'm cheating the system. I've been told all my life that working hard leads to success, and I believed it—I liked working hard and being that guy. But here's the truth: there are millions of construction workers and laborers who work much harder than you or me, and they're broke.

Don't glorify the hustle. It doesn't get you the life you want.

Creating Salesmen, Not Owners

I've worked in the real estate industry for decades—first as an investor, then as an agent, and now as a coach—and it does not teach people how to be business owners. Ninety percent of real estate coaching focuses on sales and how to get more clients.

Being a good salesperson is important, especially when you're starting out as an agent, but it isn't the only skill you need. It's like training someone to be a cook and then putting them in charge of a restaurant. No matter how good a chef they are or how many cooking classes they take to level up their culinary skills, the enterprise will fail because cooking is only one function of a successful restaurant.

It's the same with agents. You can get better at lead gen, marketing, door knocking, and hand-to-hand and belly-to-belly conversations, but as long as you only focus on sales, you will never truly progress. It takes much more to be successful and *stay* that way.

Before I niched out into real estate coaching, I used to be a business coach. One of my clients was a national energy company that was highly focused on sales. During my time with them, I got a close-up view of how they motivated their sales team.

Their sales philosophy could be summed up in one line: *get our salespeople into debt so that they're motivated to sell*. Their aim was to persuade new recruits to buy an expensive car. They worked hard to encourage this purchase. Their Head of Sales drove a fancy ride, they talked about the incredible lives the top salespeople were living—in short, they glorified wealth and status.

Sure enough, most new recruits bought the flashy car, partly because they were hooked on the image of wealth and partly to fit in. But they couldn't actually afford the car, so they went into debt to get it. Debt created motivation to sell. Those recruits needed to hit their monthly targets to pay back their loans. To sustain their lifestyle, they needed to *exceed* their monthly targets.

This business strategy is by no means unique to this energy company. Several businesses push their employees into debt so that those employees are motivated to sell. This company didn't care whether their salespeople were living a great life or reaching their potential. They just wanted to keep them on the sales treadmill.

You can see the same old-school, boiler room sales tactics at work today in the real estate industry. Brokerages know that if you keep making sales, you're not going to leave. And that's their aim: to keep you working with them and earning for them.

For the record, I have a lot of friends who are brokers. They're good people. The problem is systemic—brokerages operate on a subscription model. Netflix doesn't care how often you use your Netflix subscription or what you use it for; they just need to give you enough good content to collect their subscription fee every month. Brokerages operate on the same principle: their business model is about retaining an agent and doing whatever it takes to keep them getting sales.

This is why you're trained to be a salesperson. This is why the industry celebrates sales, not earnings. The whole industry is based on encouraging agents to sell more and more so that it can keep turning.

GCI versus Net Profit, and the Problem with Awards

It's natural to aim for awards and great to feel like you're winning. But awards in the real estate industry perpetuate the selling cycle we described in the previous section: they glorify the achievements of salesmen, not business owners.

Think about it. How many real estate awards celebrate net profit? None. Every one celebrates gross revenue—in other words, your gross commission income (GCI). When brokerages ask you for a financial goal, they frame it in terms of GCI. When award ceremony hosts hand out trophies, they celebrate GCI. The whole industry focuses on these big, grand numbers so they can hide how broke everyone is and encourage more selling.

Imagine two real estate agents, John and Bob. John has just earned a GCI of $400,000. He's kept his costs to about 25 percent, so that gives him a net profit of $300,000. Limiting costs to 25 percent is incredible in this industry and shows astonishing business acumen. To me, John has crushed it.

Now consider Bob. Bob has made a GCI of $800,000 this year. Impressive, right? That's double what John made. But Bob's costs are 62.5 percent, so his net profit is actually $300,000—exactly the same as John's. Both agents are taking home the same amount of money.

But here's the problem: in the eyes of the industry, Bob is a *god*. He is winning all the awards. Agents stop him in corridors and ask him how he did it. He's pulled up on stage to give a lecture about his strategies and how he earned this brilliant $800,000 GCI. And in that lecture hall, in the audience, is John. He's made exactly the same amount of money as Bob, but not only is he not receiving awards, but *he doesn't even know*. He's listening to Bob talk and feeling bad about his $400,000 GCI. He believes he's failed, even though he's ten times the businessman Bob is.

Awards are great. In my opinion, we should always shoot for the stars. But right now, real estate awards are manipulative. They're hosted by brokerages that want you looking at that big shiny number so you chase more sales. Brokerages themselves don't celebrate GCI. Do you know what they hand out awards for? Net profit. They're celebrating how much they make *after* they subtract operational costs, rent, and other expenses. If they didn't, they would be broke. They understand that net profit is what drives a business.

This is a fundamental, non-negotiable business principle. Have you ever seen *Shark Tank*? If you haven't, I highly recommend it; it's an excellent reality show on entrepreneurship. On *Shark Tank*, different entrepreneurs pitch their companies to three business titans—called Sharks—in hopes that the Sharks will partner with them.

If an entrepreneur on the show says he has made a million dollars, the first question the Sharks will ask him is how he has reached that figure. What are his costs? What is his net profit? In the world of business, these are white belt questions, but in real estate, they're going unasked. Imagine if that entrepreneur admitted he'd spent $980,000 to get that GCI of $1 million. He'd be laughed off the stage. The Sharks would tell him he's an awful manager and a high-risk investment.

In the real estate industry, we'd give him an award.

I hope you're seeing the very real problem with the functioning of this industry. What we celebrate grows. As long as we focus on GCI and big sales numbers, we're trapped in the hustling loop. Agents will keep not paying taxes, letting their bookkeeping fall apart, ignoring every signal that they're actually broke—as long as they keep hitting sales targets.

Instead, let's celebrate net profit. Let's celebrate how many hours in the day you're *not* working but still making money. Let's celebrate your marriage lasting. Let's celebrate the times you can take a month off to be with your newborn child while your business still makes money. Let's talk about how many referrals you get each year. Let's do all this rather than focusing purely on how many sales you make.

The Cost of Burnout

I f you have the mentality of a worker or a hustler, you're at high risk of burnout.

Imagine you have ten buyers and ten listings, which is a great number. You're working hard, maybe fifteen hours a day. You're tired, but you power through. Already, your family is wondering where you are, and you're taking long phone calls with clients while at dinner with friends. In short, your life is hectic.

But because this industry celebrates growth, you're convinced you're not doing enough. You push for more sales and that shiny award. The world aligns in your favor: there's another lead on a buyer, or a builder wants to meet you, or all of a sudden, there's a relocation company on the other side of town that wants to send you leads. Your number of clients skyrockets. Your sales figures look great. In the world of the hustlers, you've won.

But now you're exhausted. You're working more hours than you can count, and your body has no time to rest and recover. There's absolutely zero time to work *on* the business because you are a slave *to* the business. You've stopped going out for dinner with friends, and your "family time" is a quick goodnight kiss before you head back to work. You've stopped prospecting because you're trying to keep up with your current clients. And *still*, you can't complete everything on your to-do list. You fall behind.

Soon, you start to lose traction. Your clients slip through the cracks due to a lack of follow-up and long-term retention systems. One by one, they start going elsewhere. One day, you realize your phone is not ringing anymore. There are no referrals, which would have tided you over during times when you weren't prospecting. There's nothing left to do but wait for the next spring market, when you can start this feast-and-famine cycle all over again.

I've worked with hundreds of real estate agents who are facing burnout because they followed the path we're told to follow: more sales and more hustle. But this business model is broken. Hustle and sales alone will not lead to long-term success; they will eventually lead to a cycle of burnout, feast and famine, and broken relationships.

Burnout is especially scary because it can't be fixed quickly. It pushes you to question whether you want to be in this industry at all, or whether agenting is for you. These thoughts may have no basis in truth—they may be your exhaustion talking—but you don't know that. If you end up quitting the industry for a while and subsequently coming back, building momentum again can take months. You could lose six to nine months of revenue because you didn't take care of yourself or your business.

That's the very real cost of burnout: less money. And quitting isn't the only risk; you also lose money when you're functioning at half-energy. Exhaustion robs you of your charisma and motivation; it becomes harder to keep old clients and find new ones.

Guarding against burnout should be your number one priority. Before I sold my real estate team, we actually included a clause about burnout in our contracts. If it looked like someone on our team was running low on energy or they were beginning to burn out, we forced them to take a holiday. We covered all their sales. We made sure they took the time to rejuvenate because we understood that being at 100 percent energy was critical. No one on our team burned out—the cost was too high.

The Longest Sales Cycle

If you still believe hustling and pushing yourself to the limit with a sales-first mentality is the best way to succeed, allow me to remind you of another crucial aspect of the real estate business; the length of the sales cycle. I've been in sales for decades, selling everything from chocolates to Christmas lights, office furnishings to drugs (when I was on the street). Real estate has one of the longest sales cycles of any industry I know.

In a shop, for example, the sales cycle is short. They entice you with advertising, you step into the store, choose something you like, give them money, and walk out with your purchase. Simple, sweet, and short.

Real estate, however, is different. You meet someone in a grocery store while waiting to pay the cashier. You hit it off, discover that they're looking to move into a new home next year, and set up a search for them. The next year comes around and you follow up. They agree to shop around for houses with you, and if they like one, they'll buy. You show them ten or fifteen houses. Their lives get busy and they stop searching for a month. Then you notice their dream home has popped up on the market, so you get back in touch. They like it, you negotiate the offer and then write it up. If everything goes well, you finalize it. They move in and discover the house has a few maintenance or appliance issues: maybe the dishwasher isn't working or the tap leaks. You keep them happy by fixing those problems. Then, and only then, can they be considered clients for your referral base; and even then, you will need systems in place to sustain the relationship for the next twenty years.

This is a *long* cycle. From meeting someone to counting them as part of your referral base takes a minimum of ninety days—and there's about the same length of time between the first meeting and money hitting your bank account. Most real estate agents don't understand this: they think they should be seeing results immediately and get frustrated when they don't. If you have a lull in your business, don't think about what you did last week. Think about what you did *ninety* days ago because that's when you created the results you're seeing today.

This is why it's so important to snap out of the hustler and salesman mentality. This is not purely a sales business. You may need to be a salesman in the beginning, but after that, you need to form a connection with your client to make sure they stick around. This isn't just about convincing someone to open their wallet and pay you. You have to forge an authentic relationship with them so you keep them for six months, a year, twenty years. How do you do that?

And all of the above is based on a relationship with just one client. How can you scale your results with many clients? If you're running a successful business, then you likely have about 200–400 relationships minimum: how do you ensure each client loves you and keeps referring you?

It all comes down to systems. Long-term retention systems will help you serve your clients and continue to sell while your business does the work for you. They will help you keep clients for twenty years. But to *put* those systems in place, you need to make the shift from being a hustler to becoming a business owner. You have to change your mentality.

If you don't want to keep your clients and just want to sell your heart out in an endless hustle, no problem. You can make $200,000–$500,000 a year. But don't expect a strong referral base, a deep connection with the people closest to you in life, and enough time to actually enjoy any of the money you're making. To me, that's a cost that's not worth paying.

Exercise: Time Audit

Time is one of the most important assets you possess. A hustler always struggles to keep up with their business because they've run out of time. Once you make the shift to thinking like a business owner, however, you will never run out of time again.

A good, practical exercise to begin this transition from less time to more time is a time audit. I always tell my real estate clients that self-awareness is the best strategy they can adopt. You need self-awareness to understand how you function, what slows you down, and what elevates you. In short, you need to know yourself to change yourself.

A time audit reveals exactly how you're using the hours in your day so you can decide what is an effective use of your time and what's a waste. Once you identify the tasks that drain you, you can outsource them to create more time for yourself.

Here's how the audit works. Set alarms for each hour of the day, from the moment you wake up to the moment your head hits the pillow again. Each time an alarm rings, stop what you're doing and write down what you did for the past hour. You don't need to write an essay, just a few lines that capture what you did. Make sure you keep a dedicated journal for this or type it up in one place on your phone, because our aim here is to create an accurate picture of your workday and your workweek. When you've done this exercise for a while, you should be able to look back at big chunks of time and have clear visibility on how you spent them.

This bird's-eye view will show you clearly what tasks can be outsourced to create more time. It will also reveal your progress in your journey toward becoming a business owner. When I first started auditing my time, I was still focused on growing my business. I would ask myself, *how can I be more efficient every minute of every day?* I still ask myself this question, but the answer has changed. Efficiency now is getting a massage with my wife or going for a walk with my daughter. When I think about optimal performance, I no longer focus exclusively on making money. Instead, I focus on the quality of my life.

Get Your Black Belt

No matter what anyone tells you, real estate is not simply a job; it is absolutely a business. When you're doing a job, you concentrate on fulfilling one function. Within real estate, there are multiple roles: marketing, HR, tax planning, bookkeeping, customer care, buying and selling property. You cannot succeed in this profession or get the life you dream of by staying a hustler and a salesman. You must progress to becoming a business owner.

Hustlers work as many hours as they can, and they take what's left over to find some enjoyment in their life. Business owners craft a life first and then build a business to serve that life. Doing this the wrong way will cost you your relationships. It almost cost me my marriage, and it disconnected me from my kids. I didn't have anything left over to give my family and to start living a life that I loved. It's only when I changed how I thought and began hiring that my life turned around.

Allow me to address one more objection that I sometimes hear from coaching clients. They tell me they can handle the admin of their business on their own, using client relationship management software (CRM). But a CRM is actually a great example of why it's impossible to do everything alone. We all know how essential a CRM is in real estate. It keeps track of your clients' names and information, what makes them happy, their favorite food or drink, and the last time you touched base with them. It is, in essence, your list, which makes it an absolutely crucial management tool and possibly the greatest business asset you have.

But a CRM is wasted in the hands of a salesman. How do you use your CRM? Let me take a guess. You begin setting it up but abandon it halfway through. Or if you do set it up, you forget to update it. After a while, you stop using it because the information is outdated. This is why you need to think like a business owner and hire someone else to manage your CRM. You *need* an administrator to get the most out of your CRM and keep it functioning properly. It's the only way to build a business: outsource the work you're not good at so you have time to do what you do well.

If there's one takeaway I want you to remember from this chapter, it's this: you cannot outwork this industry. No matter how hard you try, your to-do list will get longer and longer. The more clients you win, the more administrative tasks will land on your desk, and the more you will fall behind. Your service levels will drop, and you will push yourself to burnout. Any business or traction you've built by working yourself to the bone, you will lose it all.

Hustlers have a white belt in business. Business owners with good systems and a great team are the people with black belts. Without help, you can grow only so much.

If you want to live a small life, stay a salesman. If you want to live a big life, filled with the freedom you dreamed of when you got your license, there's only one path that will get you there, and that's the path of the business owner.

How My New Way of Thinking Revolutionized My Business

When I think about my younger self driving all night on January 1 for a meeting that didn't happen, I find him ridiculous. I can't believe I sacrificed so much for so little.

Today, I do more than that Ben. I lead the top national team in Canada while simultaneously running a coaching company. I take walks on the beach with my wife. I plan dates with my five children. I host two podcasts, travel six to seven times a year, take on speaking engagements, run personal growth retreats, and I'm writing this book.

But the thing is, I still have more time than when I was a hustler. A lot of people ask me how I do so much, but it's a flawed question. Would you ask the owner of Walmart that question? The answer is obvious: he hired. He built a business.

If you want to be more than a flash-in-the-pan success, if you truly want to build a life you dream of, then you must become a business owner. You shouldn't be a slave to your profession; this isn't how it's meant to be. Your business should serve you, not vice versa.

I promise you, once you free yourself from a hustler mentality, possibilities will open up. You'll have more time to live the life you love. You can take the holidays you've dreamed of and focus on what fulfills you. And while you're out there living your dreams, your business will keep making you money.

Today, I spend my New Year's with my family. I create time for what I care about. And when people ask me how I do so much, I think to myself, *there's so much more I'm going to do*. Because in the life I've built for myself, there is always time to dream.

5

How to Hire

The time was 2:00 a.m. I was sitting in my back office, trying to balance my business's books. I was so absorbed in the task that I was hardly aware of how late it was. The rest of my family was asleep; I hadn't even noticed them slipping off to bed. Even at such a late hour, I wasn't even close to completing the task.

Spending the entire night bookkeeping wasn't my idea of fun, but I thought I didn't have a choice. I was not born with many natural talents. I'm not academic, I'm dyslexic, and I have ADD. But one thing I've always been able to do is work hard. Man, could I put in the hours. In my mind, working hard was my trump card.

I thought this was great news because my father, and seemingly the rest of the world, told me that if I worked hard, I would find success.

I believed that message and worked, and worked, and worked. In doing so, I missed sleeping next to my wife. I tuned out of conversations with my kids. They started conversations with me and I took an interest for a while, then stopped listening, reached over, and continued working while they were still talking. I remember my son disappearing like a ghost. Many times, we were in the middle of a conversation and I worked as he talked, thinking I could multitask, but when I looked up again, he had gone. He knew I wasn't listening, so why bother trying to talk to me?

But it was okay, right? I was building a life for my family, using my greatest skill: hard work. Eventually, I would create independent wealth. Eventually, I would be able to take care of them, once and for all. That was how I justified my obsession with work. So I stayed laser-focused on the business, delaying happiness, time with my wife, and memories with my kids. Yet, nothing got easier. The to-do list never ended. I remember writing out different lists of what needed to be done and asking myself, *what pile do I attack first? There are not enough hours in the day.* But I still believed I could outwork the endless flow of tasks.

The pressure I was under was immense. People didn't notice because I was very good at hiding it, but I was cracking under the strain. Inside my head, it was chaos. It didn't matter how good I looked when I presented to my clients or how sharp my speeches were, I was drowning in anxiety and fatigue. At my core, I'm not an angry person, but I was raising my voice, losing my temper, frustrated by even the smallest things. Adding to the pressure was the feeling that I was failing as a husband and a father. Despite these warning signs, I told myself all the hard work would pay off.

There were so many things I did then that I shouldn't even have attempted. As a dyslexic with ADD, I should *not* have taken responsibility for balancing the books. It was a ridiculous idea. In the end, I did a reasonable job, but it took me ten times longer than it would have taken a trained accountant or even someone who naturally had a head for detail and numbers. The entire time, I felt like I was writing with my left hand. And for what? I didn't realize it at the time, but I could have hired a bookkeeper for $500 a month. We were running a million-dollar company. We had properties all over the province and over twenty investors—we were big. In my head, however, we were only starting out. I couldn't convince myself we could afford a bookkeeper. So I stayed up past 2:00 a.m., battling with the books myself.

I wish I had learned that I could hire years earlier than I did. I wish I had outsourced those books to an assistant or accountant, slept next to my wife, talked to my kids, and lived the life I wanted. Because here's the truth: everything I was chasing was already right there, next to me, waiting for me to wake up and enjoy it.

Hard work is indispensable when you're starting, but as a business owner, it's not as important as you may think. If you want to scale your business, you must learn to buy other people's time.

Hiring and
Your Limiting Mindset

I n this chapter, I'm going to convince you that you need to hire an assistant, and teach you how to do it. Sounds simple, right? It is, and it isn't.

When I tell real estate agents they need to hire, it is a powerful psychological trigger. Almost every one of their limiting beliefs immediately comes into play, and they create a litany of excuses to explain why hiring is not the right decision for them right now. But it *is* the right decision, no matter how far along you are in your business journey.

You want to know why I've dedicated one-sixth of this book to something as simple as hiring someone? Because it's a total game changer. I wish I could walk you through every single story of one of my clients who has hired an assistant and show you how much time and money it saved them. Later in this chapter, I will share several stories. Hiring is the single best decision you can make, and it will determine whether or not you create a seven-figure business.

The actual process of hiring is easy: all you need is an ad and a few days. There are thousands of talented people out there, excited to give you their time and receive compensation for their work. They want to be part of something. When you hire them, you will free up time to enjoy the wealth you've created and simultaneously engineer more capacity for growth.

To actually begin the hiring process, however, you will need to get past your limiting beliefs. That's what we will tackle in this chapter. First, we will work through the excuses you tell yourself about why you can't have an assistant. Then we will give you a step-by-step process for hiring that's so simple that you can't pretend you don't know how to do it. In short, we will work through your resistance so that you hire the right person, free up your time, and skyrocket your growth.

Before we dive into the chapter, I want you to think about the subtitle of this book: *How to Build a Seven-Figure Business without Sacrificing Your Relationships*. If you're reading these pages, you have big goals. Hiring an assistant is a crucial step toward hitting those targets. Think about it: if you believe you're going to be that successful, shouldn't you be prepared for it? You can approach your business on defense and save as much as you can on your way to the top. Or you can plan to win the game and put the pieces in place to ensure success. The right team is an essential piece of the puzzle.

As much as you think knowledge is the road to power, you don't need to learn more. You need to take action. If you read this chapter and don't do anything with it, then you're wasting your time and mine. I'm not interested in you reading this book, putting a nice review on Amazon, and then doing nothing with what you've learned. What would make me happy is a review telling me that you took action and reaped the benefits. Enough learning—make the change you want to see.

Why You Won't Hire an Assistant

When I ask real estate agents to hire an assistant, they usually hit me with three objections:

* I don't have enough money.

* I don't have enough business.

* If I hired someone, what would I get them to do?

These excuses remind me of my kid opening the fridge and saying, "Dad, there's nothing to eat." Now, we usually keep a well-stocked fridge, so this always strikes me as a strange claim. Sure enough, when I get up and look at the fridge with him, there is plenty of food. There are apples, there's bread and cheese for a sandwich, some cold cuts, he can make pasta. But everything I offer him, he finds a problem with. The apples are bruised. He's not in the mood for a cheese sandwich. He doesn't want *that* cold cut. Clearly, the problem isn't that there is no food; the problem lies with him. In his negative mindset, nothing is right.

The same principle applies to agents and hiring. The three excuses above are surface-level expressions of a deeper mental block. Acknowledging this is the first step to breaking down these excuses. Once you know your resistance isn't practical, you can start tackling your deflection tactics.

Let's go through each of these excuses now so that you can pack them away once and for all.

Believing you don't have enough money to hire an assistant is a belief supported by the industry, so it's natural that you would think this. The real estate industry says you must close a certain number of deals—and, therefore, bring in a certain amount of income—before you can hire.

But the truth is, you have enough money right now. Many of the agents who tell me they're too broke to hire are holding a $6 Starbucks coffee *as they say the words.* Their Instagram profile is full of pictures of nice steak dinners that cost them $80. They've bought a new car, and now they're dropping $600 on car payments each month, but somehow they still believe that they don't have enough cash to hire an assistant.

It costs you $15–$20 to buy sixty minutes of someone's time. This is probably the most exciting fact in business. Imagine if I came to you, told you I was excellent at building companies, and I was willing to give you an hour of my time, each day, to help you out.

What would you say? You'd be pumped! One hour of my time per day to streamline your business is a great deal. So why won't you take the same step with an assistant, someone who brings a different skillset to the company than you do and who can help you grow?

The second excuse is a variation of the first: it stems from the idea that you must have a certain amount of business before you can hire. This is the most disempowering belief I've encountered because it stops people from getting the help they need *to* grow. An assistant makes your journey to the top easier and increases your capacity. You need to get one as soon as possible.

Let's say you listen to standard industry wisdom and wait until you have "enough business." You struggle to reach this point, sacrificing family time and the things you want to do, but finally you get there. You reach that arbitrary business size and today's the day. Today's the day you have *finally* suffered and struggled enough to hire an assistant. But now you're too *busy* to hire an assistant because at its current size, *your company takes up all of your time*. If you're in business, you have enough business. Hire the help you need today.

The final excuse is the most interesting: *If I hire an assistant, what would I get them to do?* The answer to this question is so obvious that it's fascinating that real estate agents don't immediately think of it. You hire an assistant to move forward. That's it. They're there to help create capacity and push your company to the next stage. In fact, they are essential to achieving this. Why would you *not* hire?

Your Psychological Triggers

Now that we've got these surface-level excuses out of the way, let's dive beneath the surface. What is the psychology behind believing you don't have enough money or business or that you won't have any work for an assistant? What is really holding you back?

With many of my clients, I find that they're perfectionists. They are scared of hiring someone because they fear that they won't be satisfied if they don't perform the task themselves. This belief is also wrapped up in fears about their communication and leadership skills. They worry they won't be able to clearly communicate what they want. And if they're a bad communicator and a poor leader, why would anyone work for them?

Many people also associate a lot of guilt with hiring. As we saw in Chapter 1, a *lot* of people have a hard time asking for help. If this is you, hiring someone can make you feel bad because they're working for you and you believe you're cheating the system.

Many of my clients also struggle with the idea that they'll be accountable to an assistant once they hire one. An assistant is like a fitness coach: you have someone calling you every day and checking in. In the case of your assistant, they ask what you want them to do. This can be petrifying. It may expose the chaos that lies under the hood of your business and your lack of effective systems.

An assistant also holds you accountable for your own tasks. If they have something on their list that needs to be done but they can't tick it off until you finish another task, they will call you to check whether you've done it. If you're a procrastinator, this is terrifying. You don't want to be held accountable for your weaknesses.

But this type of exposure is good. You *want* to take a good, honest look at the places where your business is disorganized, so you can fix the cracks. Many agents hate introducing an assistant to chaos. They want to organize their business perfectly before they hire someone. How silly is that? It's like brushing your teeth before seeing a dentist for a teeth cleaning.

Accountability is a key reason people hire a business coach. So many agents pay me thousands of dollars to hold them accountable to their business. Remember the agent from Chapter 2 who just wanted me to kick his ass to motivate him? If you're looking for accountability, hiring an assistant is one of the best ways to get it.

Last, agents don't hire because they're people pleasers. They don't want to fire someone if it doesn't work out or call them out for not doing their job effectively, so they avoid hiring entirely.

At face value, I know you don't believe you have the time or money to hire, but the factors listed above are what you are really afraid of.

These are your psychological triggers and the root causes of your resistance. Simply acknowledging them is a powerful first step. Self-awareness is necessary for change.

We live in a world where it is difficult to be real. It's a world of fake posts on social media, fake eyelashes, fake tans, fake happiness, and flashy pictures in front of Lamborghinis. And even though everyone knows it's a little bit fake, it gets celebrated.

In the real estate industry, it's hard to be vulnerable and admit that you have some chaos in your life. It's hard to say, *yes, my business has issues, but I'm letting you in so we can fix it together.* This industry teaches you to always look like a professional. You spend every second of every day telling clients you're the best option, you've got it together, you're streamlined. Your website is flashy, your business cards are perfect. Hiring can expose the fact that behind all the fancy, polished branding, there's a less polished reality. It can reveal that the whole company is just one burned-out individual, struggling to keep it together.

But that's okay. You're not alone. And in my opinion, you are never as far gone as you think. I've seen clients hire an assistant and watched problems they thought were totally overwhelming disappear within a week. Suddenly, they're right on track and they can't believe how simple it was. Get the help you need. If you don't, you will just limit your growth.

A MINDSET SHIFT:
The Project Hire

Here's a very simple hack to move past your excuses and psychological triggers. Most agents don't hire because they think about hiring on a grand scale. They wonder whether to hire someone full time or part time, what processes the new hire needs to take over, and other big questions. Before long, they're overwhelmed by the thought of hiring and training someone new. They see hiring as such an elaborate process that they never get started.

But the trick to overcoming your psychological fears without spending ten years in therapy is simply to move forward. It's exactly the same process as managing your fear: you need to educate your brain with new data so it can understand the world differently. The key to moving forward is to no longer frame hiring as an elaborate process but to instead think of it on a project basis.

Pick something you don't want to do: that's one project. It could be submitting your paperwork, getting feedback forms, or making customer service calls. Once you have a project in mind, hire someone for one hour every day to tackle that task.

There are plenty of talented people who, for one reason or another, are looking for flexibility in their jobs. Maybe they have a family to whom they want to dedicate time. Maybe they have a creative project of their own they want to focus on. Either way, there will be plenty of people with the right skills who are delighted to be hired and to make a contribution to a flourishing business.

A project hire cuts through many of your excuses. You don't need a lot of money: only $15–$20 for an hour per day. You don't need to train this person on all your processes: you only need to teach them how to execute one task. Nor do you worry about what they're going to do because you've already outlined the job.

And best of all, you move forward, giving your brain new information on hiring. Once you hire, you'll realize that buying one hour of someone's time frees up three to four hours of *your* time because your assistant is faster than you. This is their skillset.

This is the first piece of advice I give any real estate agent hesitant to hire: Change how you think about hiring. Go for the simple project hire.

How to Hire an Assistant

In the last section, we discussed some of your excuses and psychological triggers about hiring. In this section, I'm going to give you practical tips to move forward with the hiring process.

As I've mentioned already, the most important step here is to take action. It's impossible to work through all your psychological triggers before you begin: if you try, it will take you years. But simply starting can help you to work through them as you go. Remember, we want to re-educate your brain with new data. Once you hire successfully and you see what a great asset an assistant is, your brain will interpret the situation in a new light. The next time you need to hire, fewer of those psychological triggers will activate, and your brain will be on board with the process.

I really cannot hammer this point home enough: action is everything. Right after you finish reading this chapter, I want you to execute on what you have learned. Right *now*. Not next month or next year. Immediately.

The first step toward hiring an assistant is making the mindset shift toward a project hire, which we've described above. This shift will make the whole process less overwhelming: it's like the difference between trying to clean out your entire house to refreshing your closet.

The next question most people ask is, "Okay, how do I execute on making a project hire?" It's straightforward, but there is room for error, so I've devised a painless process, consisting of eleven steps, to help you take action now. Let's go through the steps in turn:

1. Conduct a Task-by-Task Energy Audit

Your first step is to identify the tasks you want to outsource—what is your project? You accomplish this with a task-by-task energy audit. I use this exercise with my clients in my real estate boot camp, and the aim is to discover which tasks drain their energy and which tasks give them energy.

Write down every task you perform in your business, no matter how small. If you put up your own signs, write it down. If you submit your own paperwork or pick up the phone, add those to the list, too. Once you have a list of every single thing you do, ask yourself three questions for each task:

- Does it strengthen me?

- Does it drain me?

- Is it neutral?

This process will help you build self-awareness. You will have a clear list of the tasks that drain your energy and therefore what you need to outsource to an assistant.

As you know from Chapter 2, operating at full energy is vital to creating a seven-figure business. If you're doing too many tasks that drain your energy, that is a 911 situation. You *must* outsource, and a task-by-task energy audit is the first step to identifying exactly what you need to delegate.

2. Create a Job Description

Once you know which tasks you want to outsource, create a job description for your assistant based on those tasks. For example, if your task-by-task energy audit has revealed that you hate paperwork, then you're looking for someone who is good at paperwork. Keep it simple and point by point. If you have identified more than one task you'd like to outsource, create an additional job description for the second, third, etc.

Don't create a list of a hundred tasks you want your assistant to do. That will be overwhelming for them and won't work for your first hire. Keep it simple and focus on a few things they can take off your plate. Remember, this is a project hire; you're not looking for them to run your entire business.

3. Decide on Their Wages and Hours

Most agents get stuck deciding what to pay their assistants. I won't tell you exactly how much to pay because rates will differ drastically depending on where you live (and how long after publication you're reading this book). I recommend taking a look at your area and checking the average per-hour rate. But I can tell you that you'll likely need to pay less than you think. It's a project hire, so it is a simple task. Hire at a slightly lower rate than you can afford so you have room to increase your assistant's wages and perhaps reward them with a bonus. If they do a fantastic job, you can even give them gifts; there are many ways to pay people.

Keep in mind that you're not looking for someone who needs the money to survive. Candidates for a project hire are usually looking for bonus money. They want independence and an opportunity to add value to an organization. This is great because you don't have the pressure of feeding someone's children.

So what hours do you hire for? I've found—and it's an amazing hack—that between 9:00 a.m. and 2:00 p.m. is the perfect time for those looking for flexible work. It gives parents time to drop their kids off and still be home when they get back from school. By hiring between 9:00 a.m. to 2:00 p.m., you're giving them hours that fit their life.

4. Don't Insist on Real Estate Experience

At this point in the process, most of my clients ask me whether they should be looking for an assistant with real estate experience. My answer is no. I've hired many people in my company, and most of them didn't come from a previous position in the real estate industry.

Think about it: if you're hiring on a project basis for tasks that drain your energy, they're usually not real-estate-specific tasks. More often than not, you're looking for an administrator. An administrator can learn processes in any industry lightning fast. Paper is just paper and software is just software, no matter the industry.

If you are thinking about getting a licensed assistant, I don't recommend going down that road. If you do hire a licensed assistant, you will want to put them in a sales position. The whole point of hiring an assistant is to get your company's admin and processes running smoothly. The moment you have your assistant opening up lockboxes and showing homes, you've lost your administrative team and your processes will start to disintegrate.

If the tasks on your list require a licensed assistant, you might be in need of a buyer's agent instead.

5. Hire as a Contractor, Not an Employee

I suggest hiring your assistant as a contractor. Think of this like hiring a photographer to showcase your properties. You wouldn't make this person an employee, would you? It's the same with your assistant. Since they're doing part-time work, a contractor role suits them better. This way, you can write them a check or transfer their payments on a monthly or biweekly basis. For taxes, all you need to do is tell your accountant to write them off.

Hiring your assistant as an employee is much trickier. If they are performing only a few tasks, I wouldn't recommend it, especially for your first hire. You will need to set up processes to deduct tax, and address numerous other considerations. If the hire doesn't work out, it may be complicated to let them go. You're welcome to chat with your bookkeeper and accountant to see what they recommend, but in my experience, hiring as a contractor is always easier.

6. Prefer Two Part-Time Assistants to One Full-Time

What if you've conducted your task-by-task energy audit and discovered a lot of tasks you want to outsource—too large a role for one part-time employee? Should you hire a single full-time employee, or is there another better approach?

In this scenario, I always recommend hiring two part-time employees for a couple of reasons. The first is to prevent a single employee from becoming overwhelmed by more tasks than they can handle; the second is so that the success of your business does not depend entirely on one person. If you hire one person to support you and they leave or you fire them, that will put your business at risk, potentially costing you thousands of dollars in lost revenue while you train someone new. If you employ two or even three people, you can set them different tasks and cross-train them. This is an essential security blanket.

7. Decide Where Your Assistant Will Work

I know this looks like an easy question with an easy answer—and it is—but this is a question I get asked a lot. More importantly, many people get stuck on these types of questions and use them as a reason not to hire. Deciding whether to hire a contractor or employee, one person or two, where they will work from—all of these are small, practical questions with simple answers. Don't let them deter you from hiring.

So where does your assistant work? Honestly, it depends on you. Do you like having someone in your office every day so they're accountable to you and can hold you accountable? Or do you work better alone in your own space? If the former, ask them to come into the office. If the latter, set up a system for remote working. There are many ways to check in with a remote employee: you can set up accountability systems, reviews, task lists, and so on to keep track of their work. Everything depends on what works best for you.

8. Know When You Need an Executive Assistant and When You Need an Admin Assistant

There are two kinds of assistants you can hire. The first is an executive assistant. This type of assistant predicts what you're going to do. As the problem solver in your business, they will often work without a preset list of tasks. In business, they are your dance partner. They will help you build out your processes and systems.

These types of assistants are expensive hires.

The second kind of assistant is an admin assistant. This is someone who says, *show me how to do it and I'll get it done.* They need a list of tasks to handle, and they will work through those tasks to lighten your load.

For a project hire, you want an admin assistant. They will be fantastic at completing the mundane tasks that drain your energy, they will always be around to pick up more work, and they are cheaper than an executive assistant. If, as your business grows, you find you need someone with more expertise, you can hire an executive assistant. But they're not a good choice as your first hire.

9. Advertise!

Now that you're clear on what kind of assistant you want, what they will do, how much you will pay them, and what hours you need them for, it is time to put an ad online. In my Real Estate Reboot Camp, we use a prewritten template that we talk participants through. But for the sake of simplification, I'm going to give you a basic framework for creating an effective ad.

First, give your ad a good title. Make sure it's eye-catching and stands out from other, similar ads. Don't just say that you're looking for help. Get specific. For example: *Looking for a world-class assistant* or *Searching for someone with incredible organizational skills.*

Second, add a disclaimer along the lines of *I will not read your résumé unless you answer the five questions at the bottom of this ad.* This is one of the greatest hiring hacks I know because it ensures people read to the end of the ad. It prevents people from spamming you with their résumés without reading what you're looking for. It also weeds out people who lack the attention to detail to answer the questions. The questions themselves can be absolutely anything. Ask applicants why they applied for the job, or how they handle learning new things. Any question will do.

After this, describe who you are. Be open and vulnerable about your business challenges, and make sure you include your mission statement. Describe your beliefs and company culture.

Next, go into detail about your ideal candidate. Be extremely specific about what you're looking for: if you can, imagine them as an avatar, a real person. Give them a name and picture the details of their life. This is a way of pinpointing your job description and the tasks you would like your assistant to handle.

Last, just before the disclaimer questions, list the hours and the wage of the role.

This framework is helpful if you're trying to compose an ad and you're stuck, but be aware that it is by no means the only way to advertise. Don't get hung up on the details: there is no wrong way to do this. Just put the ad out and get started.

10. Interview Your Short-Listed Candidates

Once you have a shortlist, the obvious next step is to interview them. Again, there is no perfect way to do this. You can jump on the phone and ask questions. You can call them for a Zoom interview. You can arrange to meet at your favorite coffee shop. The right way is the best way that works for you. Don't get hung up on the small things. Just keep moving forward and find the right candidate.

11. Re-interview after Two Weeks

One of the best pieces of advice I can give clients who are hiring for the first time is to re-interview new hires two weeks into their tenure.

When you hire someone, you'll have a reasonable idea of what they can do. But you won't know for sure whether they're the right candidate until you've observed them on the job for about two weeks. Once you've selected your favorite candidate and offered them the job, explain from the outset that you will re-interview them after two weeks. This is a simple way to check whether they're a good fit for your company.

This process benefits both you and your new hire. For you, it's easier to fire candidates who don't pull their weight. I see agents hire the wrong person and keep them for years because they can't bear to fire them. It's terrible for business. With this approach, your assistant knows they had better perform right out of the gate, and you'll be able to judge whether their work is up to scratch. If they're not bringing value to your business, you have an easy out.

The two-week interview also gives candidates a chance to re-interview you. Maybe they have questions after two weeks of working with you that weren't answered in the hiring process. Maybe there are issues they want to flag. The two-week interview gives you both a chance to have a real, honest conversation and either move forward together or part ways without animosity.

Don't Hesitate, Hire

My goal in this chapter has been to give you enough information to hire someone as soon as possible. Most people get stuck on the nuances of the process, which is why I've given you the eleven practical steps above. Some of this advice will seem obvious, but that's a good thing: it exposes how ridiculous our mental barriers can be, and how simple it is to overcome them.

In the end, you cannot understand the benefits of hiring an assistant until you do it. So do it. Move forward. It's like riding a bike; as long as you're scared of falling, you won't get on the bike to learn. But falling is just part of the process; you can't avoid it. Once you acknowledge this, you can begin learning. You have to start. If you use this eleven-step process, then you'll be learning how to ride a bike on grass, not on concrete. When you fall—*when*, not if—you won't hurt yourself.

You're not having someone take over your entire business; it's just one project. Move forward and learn as you go.

A Selection of Success Stories

At the start of this chapter, I said that if you could see how having an assistant changed my clients' lives, you would hire one immediately. I cannot describe the experience of every client I've coached, but I want to share a few success stories of people who faced unique challenges and learned new lessons from hiring an assistant. I hope you recognize yourself in one of them and that it encourages you to act.

Cory

In my early days of coaching, I worked with a client named Cory. We played squash in the mornings. Then we sat together in the hot tub and talked.

One of those mornings in the hot tub, I brought up hiring an assistant—again. Cory had been telling me he needed one for six months, yet he kept deflecting, convinced that he didn't have enough money or business. He was also particular about the way he ran his company and didn't know whether an assistant could do it right. Corey was a great agent, but he had hit a ceiling of $150,000 a year that he couldn't break through.

This time, in the hot tub, I tried a different tactic. I told him to put a free ad in Craigslist for an assistant and *not* hire. Just put the ad in and ghost people. I was trying to remove as many barriers as I could so he would at least take the first step.

It worked. He put out the ad, and once he received the applications, he actually began interviewing candidates. Before long, he hired an amazing assistant. He couldn't believe someone would work for such a small amount of money and for so few hours, but she was a mom who enjoyed getting out of the house and adding value to the company.

She now works for him for five hours a week, and the results are astonishing. He's doubled his income to over $300,000 a year. In the summer, he fishes almost every weekend and spends long vacations with his kids. This transformation started with hiring an assistant.

Peter

If you ever met Peter, he would immediately become one of your favorite people. He's a genuine, amazing human being. When Peter came to me for coaching, he had recently achieved big sales years of $300,000 and $400,000. But the previous year, he went through a divorce and earned only $100,000. He has a beautiful daughter, who has disabilities and whose needs are expensive, so his demands were different from a lot of the real estate agents I have coached.

Peter joined my coaching program to streamline his systems and get back on the horse. Pretty soon, I told him he needed an assistant. He was resistant. He was genuinely concerned he didn't have the cash, especially because he needed it to care for his child. But I knew that streamlining his systems was pointless if there was no one to help run them.

Peter needed to keep his energy free for sales. He needed to sell so the business could grow and he could bring in more money to meet his needs. But he couldn't sell if he was doing the admin for his company as well; it was draining his energy.

I told him this, and he finally agreed to try an assistant. Now he's my greatest ambassador for hiring. That simple expenditure of $500 a month pushed his business back up to $300,000–$400,000 a year and kept it there. It was an incredible turnaround. Now he's expanded to hiring a marketing assistant and other help, to the extent that he does no admin whatsoever. He's much happier, he's not burning out, he has time to spend with his daughter, and he's not worried about finances.

Peter's story is common in the real estate industry. So many agents overwork themselves, and the moment they have to stop selling for some reason (in Peter's case, divorce), the business crashes. Since hiring an assistant, Peter has not faced that crash again. There may be years he goes through personal crises, but his business has never ground to a halt. His assistant and his systems keep it going.

Jimmy

Jimmy entered the real estate business through his family: his mother was a top agent, and he took over the company from her. He joined my program to get organized, grow personally, and update his mom's systems. I asked him what I always ask: *Do you have an assistant?* Jimmy didn't, so he hired one. This one simple move made a huge difference to his life.

But here is the point of this story: Jimmy's assistant quit. This happened around the time the COVID-19 pandemic hit, and people were unsure what its impact on the real estate industry might be. Jimmy made the call that replacing his assistant wasn't necessary. He could do without.

He was mistaken. To everyone's surprise, the real estate industry boomed during the pandemic. Sales rose, inventory dropped, and the market boomed. It seemed that people were spending so much time at home that they realized they needed an upgrade. Jimmy burned the candle at both ends trying to keep up. At home, his wife had a third child right when COVID-19 hit, so he was trying to balance spending time with his wife and child with catering to his business.

Jimmy was part of my Business from Within private VIP course, which is my high-end mastermind. It's some of the most powerful work I do. We go on retreats that bond us together like family: we have breakthroughs and share. Jimmy always loved these retreats and never missed one.

This time, though, he missed it. I later learned that his relationship at home was desperately strained because he was working so much. His mental health was shot to hell, and his business was paying the price because he couldn't keep up. When I came back from the retreat and jumped on a call with him, he looked ragged. A mere six months after his assistant quit, he was exhausted and frustrated.

After a chat with me, he took three days off in a solo cabin, fully disconnected from his business. When he came back, he immediately hired a new assistant. Jimmy was burned out, so it took him time to recuperate and get back to his original energy levels. But with an assistant, he managed to reset to where he was. Now his business is booming beyond anything he could have imagined and he's reconnected with his family and his wife.

You always need an assistant. Ask Jimmy if he would do without one again and he'd tell you that the cost is simply too high.

Koukun

We've met Koukun already in Chapter 2. This time, Koukun and I were working on setting up systems for his business. He's a great real estate agent, but I told him what I tell everyone else: he needed an assistant.

He listened to me immediately. He put out an ad, interviewed candidates and hired someone he was very happy with. I was super proud. He did it! He executed flawlessly.

Within two weeks, his assistant quit.

I told him this happens and he shouldn't worry. We started the process again: put out an ad, interviewed, and hired. The second assistant *also* quit within a few weeks. This happened three more times. Koukun would hire and his assistants would quit on him.

At this point, it was clear the only common denominator was Koukun. So I sat him down and we looked at how he communicated. It was a mess: he was forgetting niceties, he was demanding, his expectations were too high. We needed to take a deep dive into the best way to connect with other human beings and function as a leader. This is a crucial lesson for every leader, and we learned how much Koukun needed it only *because* he hired an assistant.

Now, of course, Koukun is doing great. He has an assistant, he's one of the top ten agents in his brokerage, and he has a team of agents working for him, many of whom are touching sixty deals. He's been in business only five years. Koukun followed the system well, but he had to get out of his own way to truly unlock his potential.

Create Capacity for the Life You Want

This is an industry that emphasizes sales and hustle. It glorifies working hard. But the truth is, you may need hard work in the beginning, but hard work alone will only set you on a path to frustration and burnout.

To grow, you need to hire an assistant. An assistant creates capacity so that you can sell more while they take care of the admin. My advice to you is to hire an assistant *before* you need one. And don't worry about the money; you always have enough money. A good rule of thumb is to set aside 10 percent of your gross income to hire an assistant. If you make $100,000 a year, that's $10,000 for an assistant; if you make $50,000, that's $5,000. But if you make $1 million a year, you should be investing $100,000 of revenue into your admin. It's a rule of thumb, but it works.

Remember, this book is about building a seven-figure business and keeping your relationships. You're not trying to become a better salesman. You want to be a business owner so you can lead the life you love. Protect your relationships, foster deep connections, and make time for the adventures that make life worth living.

Hiring an assistant is a catalyst for that life. It unlocks the time to follow your compass, build out your business without putting strain on your wife and kids, and simply to slow down. It protects your mental health because you're not doing tasks that you hate and because you have time for the things that energize you. You can be at peace knowing you aren't letting the people in your life down.

All of this is only possible if you execute. You cannot win if you don't act. It's the fuel to everything. I know it's human nature to avoid what we don't like. As we said in the Introduction, long-game systems are like vegetables. No child wants to eat their greens. They may know it's good for them and they need those nutrients, but they still don't want to do it. Given the choice between greens and ice cream, every child will choose ice cream. The good news is that I'm not asking you to fight this tendency. I'm asking you to *align* with it. Because in business, you don't *have* to eat your greens. Your assistant will do it for you.

I want to leave you with one more thought here: hiring an assistant will unlock a huge amount of capacity, but having someone on your team doesn't negate the inner game we've talked about in the earlier chapters. In fact, it makes that inner game and mental work even more crucial, as Carson's story illustrates.

Carson was already one of the top agents in the city when he came to me: he had built a seven-figure business. I didn't know it at the time, but Carson's wife had seen me on a TV morning show talking about how my marriage almost broke up because of how hard I worked, and she asked Carson to get in touch with me. The two of them were going through a very bad patch and were separated.

When we met, Carson admitted that he was so busy at work, it was affecting his relationships at home. He thought the solution was to get an assistant, and he knew I was good at helping my clients hire. But for Carson, the situation was different. He already *had* two assistants. He had buyer's agents and a flood of business. Another assistant would buy him more time, yes, but what would he do with that time? Spend more time with his family, or fill that new capacity with more growth?

Carson joined my Real Estate Reboot Camp and realized he had no clue what he wanted: where was his compass pointing? He finally realized that he needed to create more capacity for himself but use it to build his family, not his business. His wife moved back in with him and they attended one of my personal growth retreats. He's now living the life he dreamed of when he started this business: he's bought a boat, and he's spending enough time with his daughter to build an authentic relationship. He is giving away the deals he doesn't want so he can live the life he actually wants.

Carson proves that it is absolutely essential to set your compass and know what you are aiming for. If you don't, you will make growth the main focus of your goals, and it shouldn't be. Growth is only the path to the goals.

Hire an assistant, and increase your capacity. Build that business you're dreaming of. But make sure you know how to use that capacity to get the life you want.

Invest Money to Make Money

When I entered the real estate market as an agent, I had already been a real estate investor and a coach, so I could learn from my mistakes. I hired an assistant immediately, within the first few weeks of setting up the business. It's one of the reasons why, within two years, I had earned $1.1 million in paid-out commissions. I knew how to structure my company so that I was a business owner.

All of the problems I experienced when I was doing bookkeeping at 2:00 a.m. were still there. I'm still dyslexic and ADD, and I'm still no academic. The difference now, though, is I know how to play to my strengths. When I operated as an agent, I had a team working for me because I knew I could sell—I could bring in the deals. What I wasn't good at, I outsourced. I made sure someone else was doing my admin so I had the time to concentrate on what I could crush.

In the last chapter, we imagined buying a restaurant and trying to do it all: cook, cleaner, maître d', dishwasher. Don't let that be you and your business. If you think you can do it all, you will fail.

Nor should you wait to hire help. If you keep waiting until you have "enough" money, then you will be too busy to train your assistant when the time comes. I won at the real estate agent game because I had an assistant from the get-go who could handle my systems for me. It left me free to make eight to ten sales per month and still spend time with my family. If you truly believe you're going to build a seven-figure business, *hire now*.

Asking for help is not weak. It's not wrong. I'm sitting here right now, dictating this book to my buddy Rob. He works with Scribe Media, and he's interpreting what's in my crazy head so he can put it on the page. You think, as an ADD and dyslexic person, that I would actually be able to sit down and write out a book? Not a chance. You need to find people to fill the gaps.

I am far from perfect, but I am one hell of a businessman. I know that for whatever I need, there will always be people to help me. Be a business owner. Invest the money you need to make money.

6

Keep Your
Clients for Life

When I was a real estate investor, almost none of the agents who serviced me stood out. I was a pretty big fish—I often bought ten to fifteen properties at a time, which represented at least $100,000 in commission for an agent—yet, not one agent did anything above and beyond to show me their appreciation. In most cases, I didn't even get a thank-you card.

Several of these agents had amazing marketing and stunning branding but didn't ask me a single question about myself. It seemed like they were only interested in getting me to put pen to paper; once the deal was signed, they were gone. And it made me feel like a transaction.

These experiences had an influence on how I described the agents to my friends and family. I never bad-mouthed them; after all, they did find me the properties I wanted. But I never raved about them either. Why would I? They hadn't done anything special for me.

By the time I became a real estate agent myself, I had already been an investor and a business coach, so I knew right away I was going to run my business differently from everyone else. The first thing I decided was that I wouldn't look at my clients with dollar signs in my eyes but as human beings. They were real people, with hopes, fears, and wants.

You have to remember, every potential client leads a full life. Maybe their loved one has cancer or they are worried about losing their jobs. Perhaps they are celebrating falling in love or stressing about whether their kids can get into a good school. Whatever it is, their lives are rich and meaningful. Bad shit has happened to them; so has good shit. I wanted to connect with those stories. I wanted to see them for who they were.

I know at this point you're thinking, *That's nice, Ben*, *but how does it help you build a real estate business?*

You want to know a secret? It's the absolute *best* way to build a real estate business. And I'm going to explain how with a theory from nuclear physics: the critical mass theory.

I first heard of this theory while listening to an audio CD by Wayne Dyer. (Yes, an audio CD.) It's a theory in quantum physics that refers to the critical mass a substance needs in order to sustain a chain reaction. Now, I am not the best at science or nuclear physics, but it goes something like this.

As human beings, 99 percent of our bodies are made up of atoms of hydrogen, carbon, nitrogen, and oxygen. We also contain much smaller amounts of the other elements that are essential for life. We have atoms, particles, protons, neutrons, and quarks.

Imagine a petri dish filled with everything that makes up a human, from a quantum perspective. As a scientist adds these particles to the dish, the first thing she finds is that they vibrate and have an energy of their own. The individual particles are scattered around the edge of the petri dish, so she brings some to the center and they connect like a magnet. She moves more to the center, and they start forming a group. She keeps adding more and more, until at some point—boom. They all move suddenly to the center, like a large magnet has been turned on. This is critical mass theory: eventually, there's so much force and magnetism that everyone jumps in. But it starts with one connection at a time.

We see critical mass theory at play all the time. Think about Justin Bieber and how he became famous: one view on YouTube, then twenty, then a thousand, then an avalanche. Overnight, he's a celebrity. Most movements work in the same way: one follower, then two, then fifty, then eleven thousand, and soon you can't stop the momentum anymore.

Now apply this theory to real estate. If we all have a magnetic force inside of us, as quantum physics proves, why would I *not* focus on blowing the mind of each client I meet, and let critical mass theory do the rest? This industry teaches us that marketing is the only path to sales. But as an investor, I never chose an agent based on marketing. I only worked off recommendations. So why would I not build a referral-based business?

Of course, that's exactly what I did. I didn't pump thousands of dollars into branding or campaigns. I didn't even have a business card and a website. I just found my first client, focused on making a real, human connection with them, blew their minds, and trusted that they would refer me to others. I focused on one client at a time and let the momentum build.

It worked. Within one calendar year, I had $440,000 in paid-out commissions in a city with an average of $400,000 for established agents. In my second year, I made $660,000. That's $1.1 million in two years, with *very little traditional* marketing.

My theory was right: by focusing obsessively on blowing the minds of one client at a time, with service and emotional connection, I created an experience that they could not help but share with their friends. Although I did use strategies such as door knocking, coloring contests, farming an area, doing open houses, making cold calls, and talking to strangers to get the ball rolling, my business quickly transitioned from cold sales to living off referrals. Just like the particles in the petri dish, my business created its own magnetic force. I focused on one real connection at a time, and pretty soon I hit critical mass, regularly attracting new clients.

If you want a business that doesn't depend on constant hustle, then you need to shift your focus from taking over a city and plan on going deep with one connection at a time until you hit critical mass. To do this, you need to blow your clients' minds with service and emotional connection that will last from the first moment you meet for the next twenty years. Yes, this approach will take systems and a team, but it will force you to become a business owner, not just a front-end salesman. Eventually, even the best salesman gets tired of constantly selling.

Attack or Attract: Building Your Referral Base

The best analogy I have for a transaction-based business versus a referral-based business is the game of *Civilization*. You've probably heard of it. As a kid, and even into my teenage years, I used to love that game.

The aim of *Civilization* is to—you guessed it—build a civilization. You're placed on a map, where you create a city and mine for raw materials to build your resources. As your civilization grows, you start expanding across the map.

Now, there are two ways to win at *Civilization*. You can use your resources to develop your army and make weapons. Once you have enough soldiers, you can send your army to conquer cities by force. It's bloody and tragic, but you can do it.

The second way to win is to develop your culture. You use your resources to make books, create scholars, and build libraries. Slowly, as you expand your city, your border touches the border of another city. Because you've spent time cultivating your culture, you get a notification on your screen: this new city wants to merge with you. They're *attracted* to what you're building.

Marketing is very similar to trying to win *Civilization* by building your army: you go out there and try to land sales by aggressively pushing your brand onto people. But there is another way. You can *attract* clients to your business by offering an incredible experience —by focusing on your culture—and building out your referral base from day one, one client at a time.

Think about it. If you have completed 500 transactions and you have a referral rate of 10 percent, that equates to fifty additional transactions, all without a marketing budget or any hard sell. Now imagine if this rate was even higher. Hopefully, with this type of motivation, you won't need to force yourself to talk to someone in a supermarket ever again.

Despite these staggering statistics, almost no one in real estate is focused on keeping their clients. Agents talk about it all the time, but they don't act on it. All our energies are channeled into learning the next new sales tactic, into marketing gimmicks that can catch more eyeballs, into fancy websites and flashy business cards. We've mastered the art of the hard sell, but we're not taking care of the clients we already have.

If you want to know how bad client retention is in the industry, consider your own career. Most of the clients you land through aggressive marketing have had agents before you. Most of those clients will move on to new agents after you. Almost no one is keeping their clients. Most agents don't even care. They're focused on transactions, on how many deals they can sign, not on the clients themselves.

If you want to build a real estate business that stands out, you need to focus on referrals from day one. To build out your referral base, you will need to create an experience that *matters* to the client, and you can only do that if you see them as people, not merely sales. You must focus on creating an emotional connection.

The Value of
Emotional Connection

M ost agents in this industry are good. You're competing with people who know their jobs, close deals, and can give their clients what they're looking for 90 percent of the time. So how do you stand out and get chosen?

The answer is emotional connection.

Let's illustrate the power of emotional connection using a very simple example. Imagine your mom was looking for a house and needed an agent. You're an agent. Does your mom ask around, or does she simply hire you?

Provided you have a healthy relationship with your mother, of course she chooses you! You might not be the best agent in the area, or the flashiest, or the biggest. But she will pick you every time because she has an emotional connection with you. Her decision isn't based on performance; it's based on your relationship.

Now imagine that you make a mistake. Perhaps you're a little slow to respond to a call and you lose a buyer. Will your mom yell at you and hire a new agent? Again, as long as you handle the situation professionally and have a healthy relationship with your mom, of course she won't. She'll forgive you because the two of you are connected emotionally, a bond that runs far deeper than connection through your performance as a realtor.

This is the type of connection you need to create with your clients. You must connect with them on a real level, as human beings. Flip the narrative. Don't focus on the sale; focus on them. Listen to them. Show people that you *see* them and get them. They will then associate you with the positive feelings they experience around you. Anytime someone asks for a recommendation for an agent, they will think of you.

If you can achieve this, you will be unstoppable. Think about how many people really *get* you, 100 percent. I mean people you can rely on in an instant, who know you on every level and don't misunderstand you. Most people can't name more than two or three in their lives. When I ask this same question at real estate coaching classes, many of my agents say that no one truly gets them, not even members of their own family.

Imagine the impact you could create if you could truly *get* your clients. Imagine how magnetic and powerful that connection would be. If you want to keep your clients for life, focus on their emotional needs, not merely their buying and selling needs.

Your Brand Is the Conversation
behind Your Back

To build a real estate business that meets your client's emotional needs, you must change how you think about branding.

Most agents invest a significant amount of money into marketing campaigns and flashy branding. They believe their brand is a fancy logo, a streamlined website, a wrapped car, their face on the billboards in the area. There is nothing inherently wrong with any of these marketing strategies, but they are focused on attacking, rather than attracting.

Instead, think about your brand as the conversations that happen behind your back. This is what your clients are saying about you when you're not in the room. It's how they respond when someone at a dinner party asks, *hey, I'm looking for a real estate agent. Got any recommendations?*

Never underestimate the power of the conversation behind your back. Clients talk about real estate agents all the time. Pop over to a local Facebook group or a mom's group and ask them, *who is the best agent in your area?* The answers are revealing. Many people will recommend their agents, but once in a while, you'll get a post that isn't so pretty. Someone feels like their agent cost them a ton of money. Someone else thinks their agent talked them into buying a house they didn't really want. These comments stand out like a glaring scar. Years ago, a sales trainer told me that bad news travels sixteen times further than good news. In my experience, this has proven very true.

Often, I find the agents with the most negative feedback are the ones with the most branding. I knew a real estate agent once who was absolutely crushing it in an area. Her branding was through the roof, and she always won the million-dollar award. But her clients wouldn't recommend her.

I actually know this real estate agent and she's lovely. Her heart is definitely in the right place. But she's so busy that she consistently lets her clients down. The only way she stays in business is by pouring money into marketing and securing new clients because her old ones don't stick around. She always needs to sell; she cannot get to a place where she lives off referrals.

Long-Game Systems: Set Yourself Up to Make Sales

So far, we've talked about how to adjust your mindset from a marketing-based business to a referral-based business. We've outlined the importance of emotional connection and seeing your brand as the conversations behind your back. These conceptual shifts are crucial to refocusing on the client instead of the sale, and making a great impression.

But I also want to give you practical systems that you can implement to truly blow your clients' minds and keep them for life. This is the long-game system we talked about in earlier chapters. These processes are designed to help you stand out from the crowd, make an incredible impression during a sale, and then continue to make that same impression for decades to come. To make them easy to absorb, I've broken them down according to the life cycle of a client: "Making a Sale" and "After a Sale."

Insulating Your Clients

Insulating a potential client is the first step to transforming a lead into a client. It's like pouring coffee in a thermos: when you have a hot lead, the first thing you need to do is insulate it.

Let me illustrate this with an example. Adam was on my team for years, and he met with a potential client who wanted to price her home. His potential client contacted us via a buyer's mailout we did. Everyone knows that if you've done a buyer's mailout, you're the client's third choice. The first choice is the agent they already have, the second choice is an agent someone recommended to them, and the third choice is you.

Adam is amazing: likable, smart, aware of how to make a connection and blow his clients' minds. When he went to this meeting, he absolutely crushed it. He called me on the way home to update me on how it went. There were indeed two other agents before him: the woman's existing agent and someone recommended by their mom. We were at a disadvantage. But Adam had taken the time to connect with this woman. He knew her hobbies were psychology and wine. They'd talked about her favorite orchard in California and the type of wine she loved. She liked him.

The lead was hot, but we knew it might go cold. Adam needed to insulate the lead immediately. We were still on the phone talking when he got home. I told him to drive back out, go to the nearest wine shop, pick up her favorite wine, and leave it on her doorstep. I didn't want him to ring the bell or hand it to her personally. This wasn't about him or him giving her the gift. This was about her.

The next day, the woman opened her door to find a bottle of her favorite wine on the front step and a note from Adam thanking her for the meeting. She was awestruck. She called us, in a state of high emotional charge—just filled up. It wasn't because we bought her a bottle of wine; anyone can do that. *It's because we bought her a bottle of wine connected to her story and showed her we understood what she loves and cares about. It's because we were listening.*

We ended up winning the listing and selling her house. We earned more than $8,000 in commission and gained a lifelong client.

How to Gift

Like Adam, I make sure to buy a thoughtful gift for most of the clients I meet. This is to cement our emotional connection and create a relationship. It's to show them that I get them.

We have won more real estate transactions through creating a connection where the client feels seen and heard than through any amount of marketing you can name. Most sales don't come from pricing a house well or bragging about your social media presence. People choose you because they like you. That's what happened with Adam that day. The client liked him, we were thoughtful, and we won the listing.

I cannot emphasize strongly enough how important it is that the gifts you give clients must be *thoughtful*. As I write this chapter, I'm scared many of you will think I'm telling you to just do something nice for your clients. *I buy my clients gifts, too*, you're thinking. *What's the big deal?* But the gift is not the point. The point is the meaning *behind* the gift. I once got two bottles of wine from my lawyer—I had sent him forty to fifty clients that year and he gave me two bottles of wine. I drink wine once every two years. That gift made zero impact on me. To be perfectly honest, it frustrated me, because it showed me how little he knew me.

Your gift must be *thoughtful*. The impact it has depends on how your client connects to the gift and the emotions it triggers. A gift has to say, *I hear you. I see you. And I deeply understand you.*

A few years back, I was showing first-time buyers potential houses. One woman kept pointing out wolf pictures and figurines in the houses. She absolutely loved wolves. She didn't know why, but she felt connected to them.

So I asked her about wolves. What did they mean to her and why? We spent our time together seeing houses, while I understood this topic she cared so much about. She loved it. She felt heard. Wouldn't you feel the same if someone talked to you about a topic you love? It's not a sales technique. It is a genuine way to make a connection with clients. It helps them open up.

When we signed the deal for her new home, I knew right away what I was going to get her as a gift. I went to a photo gallery and purchased a limited edition wolf print. It was massive and magnificent. It wasn't the cheapest gift I've bought, but it didn't matter. I knew it would make an impact.

When I delivered the keys to her new house, I walked through the front door with this massive picture wrapped up. When she opened it, she cried. It connected with her emotions, and it bonded us.

As humans, we feel so much emotion based on whether we feel heard or misunderstood. Each thoughtful gift can take a person back to a time when they were listened to, forging a connection with a lifetime of experiences. If you get your thoughtful gift right, you can make a lasting connection with your client.

But what if you haven't had time to get to know your client particularly well and don't know what to give them? I once had clients who bought their house very quickly: it was the second house I showed them, and the deal was signed in record time. I hardly had any time to get to know them.

In situations like this, you can still create a connection by focusing on how you deliver the gift, creating a little drama and making your gift memorable. Your aim is to create something worth talking about. For these clients, I bought five $20 gift cards. I put each card in an envelope with a short, thoughtful note. Then I wrote "Open on Day One" on the first card, "Open on Day Two" on the second, and so on.

As they moved into their apartment, I handed them these cards. I told them it was a bit of a game: one card for each day of the first five days in their new home. They absolutely loved it. Each morning, they were excited to open a card and see what it said. It became a ritual for them, a beautiful way to mark a new phase in their lives.

And so naturally, they talked about it. They took pictures of the cards, posted them on social media, and told their friends, because they were a sensitive, thoughtful, and fun gift. If you haven't had time to create a deep emotional connection with your clients, innovative delivery of a simple gift can make all the difference.

It's Not about You

If there is one thing I caution real estate agents against, it's making the gift about you. Don't deliver in a way that draws attention to yourself or makes it seem like you're asking the client to praise your innovation or thoughtfulness. Don't give them a present just because you want more sales or so that they'll refer you to their friends. It cheapens the gift and ruins the emotional connection.

The gift is about them. Honestly. Your aim is to impact someone and make them feel like they are understood. If you can focus on that when you give gifts, your presents will land. You will create relationships that last you for decades and consistently feed your business.

Red Carpet

Let's recap. The first part of making a sale is standing out from the crowd by insulating your client and then through creating a connection with them by giving them a thoughtful gift. I hope it goes without saying that this requires you to *genuinely* get to know them. It's not simply a trick or a tactic. The good news is that if you're focused on emotional connections and running everything through the filter of "my brand is the conversations behind my back," you will do this naturally.

But once you sign the deal, do something to make your clients feel special. We have a process for this; It's called the "red carpet." If you've heard about this process before, it's because it started with us and I've talked about it everywhere.

This is how it works. Buy a three-feet-by-ten-feet red carpet, along with stanchions and red rope. When your client comes to pick up their keys and visit their new home, they find this red carpet waiting for them, as though they were a celebrity, marking this grand occasion.

The impact is huge. Most clients are excited and moved—none of their previous real estate agents ever did this for them. Neighbors start coming out of their houses and asking, *what is going on?* You introduce your clients as the new owners of this house. You create incredible buzz.

The same process applies if your clients have bought an apartment. Just roll the red carpet out in front of the condo entrance. Tenants will peer out of their windows to see the excitement, and the audience will make your clients feel like royalty. It's magic.

As your clients enjoy their moment on the red carpet, take a picture. This step is crucial for another process, which we're going to talk about in the next section. But for now, get them to stand on that red carpet with a basic SOLD sign, and take a picture.

Again, don't make this about you. I see so many real estate agents asking their clients to hold SOLD signs with the agent's face on or the agent's name printed in large bold letters. Don't do this. It will cheapen the experience and ruin the moment for your clients. Remember, your brand is the conversation behind your back. Your brand *is* the experience. What will your clients say about the agent who jumped in on their special moment and tried to use it as a marketing opportunity? Focus on making the moment memorable *for your clients* so they can look back on it in years to come.

Long-Game Systems II: Post-sale Relationship Building

Most agents think that their job ends when they make the sale. Once they close one deal, they get back into the hustle mindset and redirect their energies toward new clients.

But in a referral-based business, you want your client to remember you for decades to come. You want to keep the conversation going. It's actually the after-sale processes that matter the most because these keep you in your clients' minds. This isn't a one-night stand; it's a relationship. You have to nurture it.

This is why systems matter. You can't rely on hustle when it comes to relationships: you need to work at them and build them carefully. Systems sustain a relationship with your client long after they sign on the dotted line.

The Fridge Magnet

The next part of the Long-Game System begins ninety days after you close the deal. For those ninety days, everyone is still talking about your client's new house. They're asking how it feels to move in, whether the light is right, are they happy with the location. But after around ninety days, this conversation begins to change. The house is no longer the first subject on everyone's minds. Other events take precedence. People start talking about jobs, their kid's soccer game, and the latest gossip in the neighborhood.

Ideally, you want the conversation to pivot *back* to the house now and again. You want to trigger reminders of how great it was to work with you so clients discuss it with their friends. This is why you give them the fridge magnet.

Remember that picture I asked you to take on the red carpet? Get that picture printed on a fridge magnet and send it to your clients with a warm note. Because you didn't make them pose with a branded sign, the picture serves as a reminder of a beautiful day in their lives. It's a memento they'll want to display on their fridge.

Now, this is crucial: don't brand the magnet either. Maybe put your number on the back of the magnet and slot in a business card. But that's *it*. No logo, no picture of your face smiling down at them. This is because you want to start a *conversation*. Once again, this isn't a marketing exercise—at least not in the way you're used to thinking of marketing exercises.

Let's say your clients invite someone over for a cup of tea or host a dinner party where people mill about in the kitchen. Someone notices the magnet. They think, *I wonder what this is about?* If the magnet's branded with your name and face, they'll see your logo and their question will be answered. It's another real estate agent. But if there is no brand, they may be curious enough to ask their hosts for the story behind the magnet. This will give your clients a chance to talk about the connection you made with them, the thoughtful gift you bought them, and that amazing red carpet experience. Hopefully, they'll say, "Well, *my* agent didn't do that."

The Birthday System

The birthday system is one of the best long-game systems out there. It is guaranteed to sustain your connection with clients for decades and give you a five-star review whenever they speak to someone about you.

Most real estate agents send something small to celebrate the first-year anniversary of their clients buying their home. After that, they disappear. Again, this is an agent-focused behavior. Normal people don't celebrate one year of living in a house. They celebrate actually buying the house. Have you ever been to a party to celebrate the one-year anniversary of someone moving into a house? Me neither. The only person who cares about the one-year anniversary of a house sale is the real estate agent who helped them find it.

But you know what people do celebrate? Birthdays. When you were a child, birthdays were incredible. Your friends came over, you got presents, your mom ordered your cake with whatever decoration you liked, everyone sang to you. It was, hands down, the best day of the year, because you were the center of attention. Then, after your sixteenth birthday, everything just stopped. You didn't celebrate birthdays anymore; all of a sudden, you were too old for them.

The Birthday System is designed to tap into that feeling you got as a child, when you felt special and cared for. That's why it's the most powerful system we implement in our business. It is responsible for many of the referrals we get, and it is incredibly simple to introduce.

Here is how it works. We have a standing order with a local bakery for a box of delicious, freshly baked cookies. My assistant hands me a list of people who have their birthdays this month and I check it, just to account for any clients who have died or have moved out of the city. As a business owner, that's as much as I need to do to ensure that this process runs smoothly. My assistant then takes this list to the bakery, where they enter it into their system and deliver the cookies on the relevant clients' birthdays. Every year, on their birthday, my clients open their front door to find a batch of freshly baked cookies waiting for them, with a note that reads:

Happy birthday. We just want to say how much we love you as a client and as a human. We're just so happy that we get to know you. Hopefully, this is a really great day for you.

That's it. But we do it year after year, without fail, whether or not someone has listed with us again. Every birthday, we show up.

The responses have been astonishing. I've had clients call me after four years and say, *Ben, I can't believe you're still sending me cookies on my birthday. That's incredible. There's no one else we want to list with; we tell everyone about you.* We get social media shout-outs and long messages of appreciation.

I know this sounds simple—so simple that it's hard to believe it has such an impact. But we tap into that giddy feeling people had when they were children and we give them that feeling back. I've had clients who look forward to opening their doors on their birthday because they know our cookies will be waiting for them. If there's one system you must implement, it's this one.

Other Ways to
Keep Your Client for Life

I could write an entire book on the systems we use to keep blowing our clients' minds and turn them into raving fans, but I don't have space. So instead, I will share two more ways you can stand out to your existing and prospective clients.

Christmas Drop-off

I am not a fan of Christmas gifts. To me, they feel like obligations, and those never make a real impact. Buying my wife flowers for Valentine's Day is nice, but buying her flowers on March 10 for no reason is more special.

So I don't recommend getting caught in the Christmas gift game. Almost every business your client is in touch with will send them a gift on Christmas; you'll be one among many, and you don't have time to stand out by sending something personal to everyone on your list.

Instead, orient the Christmas season toward prospective clients. This is how we do it. We collect addresses throughout the year, from January onward. Then we buy small gifts—Christmas wreaths, advent calendars, Christmas doormats—and drop them off at these addresses. We make a company trip out of it: we pile the gifts into our cars, drive around, and distribute them.

For this to work, clients need to feel that the gift was an accidental, thoughtful gesture. If your prospective client feels like you drove all the way to their place to drop off a Christmas gift, they are going to feel bad. They may feel pressured to list with you, and then the emotion associated with the gift is not "pleasant surprise" but "manipulation." We always tell them we were in the area dropping off gifts for clients, and we had a spare. This way, it's not a hard sell but a chance to make them feel good.

Once, we knocked on the door of the owner of Panago Pizza. Two years prior, he asked me to price his home, but he didn't list. When I showed up on his doorstep with a Christmas wreath, he was overcome with emotion. He told me he wasn't even sure if he was going to sell the house anytime soon. I told him it didn't matter. I appreciated being able to price his home and getting to know him.

But people want to give back. So he asked me what he could do for me. Jokingly, I said, *Well, put the wreath on your door. And if anyone comes in and asks where you got that wreath from, tell them they need to sell their house with me.* We both laughed, and then I left. But the impact was made: we did something thoughtful at an unexpected moment, without expecting anything in return. You bet if someone asks him where he got that wreath from, he's going to tell this story.

Photo Shoot

This is a simple, effective, and cheap way to create conversation among your clients, both prospective and current. We get in touch with a builder who has a beautiful home or a beautiful apartment and we ask if we can use it for one day. We bring in a photographer. Then we send a letter to our clients, informing them that on a specific date, they can come to this particular address and get a family photo shoot for free.

This approach is incredibly popular. People love to have a photo with their family, in a beautiful space, that they can use on their Christmas cards or send to relatives at any time of year. It costs you very little, it's easy to do, and it gets people talking about you. When people see that framed picture or receive a Christmas card with the family photo on it, they will ask where it was taken—and you become part of the conversation.

Create Raving Fans

I hope that by now, I don't need to reiterate the benefits of a referral-based business. Compare the value of one sale versus the value of a client who refers you for thirty years, and it's a no-brainer: one sale versus the minimum ten referrals you'll get across decades. This is the 10X industry figureheads keep talking about, yet no one focuses on client retention as a way to create it. You don't need to sell more. You need to keep your clients forever and compound your list. This way, you create more revenue and spend less on marketing.

Think back a decade or two, and you'll remember that there was a time when the world seemed to be divided into Apple or PC users. If you were a PC user, you liked your computer but you weren't crazy about it. If someone bad-mouthed Windows to you, you probably shrugged and complained along with them: there were definitely problems to complain about.

But Apple users were fanatics. They *loved* their Macs and defended them to the death. I don't know whether this is still the case, but in the time of Steve Jobs, I could say to an Apple user at a party, "I prefer Windows myself" and just watch them go off. I used to do it for fun. They would break down why the graphics were better, how the usability was unparalleled, how the hardware never crashed. They worked so hard to convince me to switch.

Those are the kinds of clients I want. I want an army of advocates who aggressively recommend me to their friends. I want people to say, *Who's your real estate agent? Fire him because he's not as good as Ben.*

How did Apple build that loyalty? It's because Steve Jobs focused, from day one, on user experience. Prioritizing his clients was paramount to him. If you want to build a referral-based business, you need to do the same.

Keeping a client for twenty years is not about gimmicks or marketing. It's a relationship based on authentic, emotional connection. You must take the time to know them and figure out what makes them tick. What makes them laugh and cry? What memories do they cherish? What do they care about?

Remember, your brand is the conversation behind your back. It's what people are saying when you're not in the room, not to your face. It's not about how fancy your website is or how many posters you have on bus benches. It's about whether you're creating experiences with your clients that they *want* to talk about.

Think about it this way. If someone came up to you on the street and gave you a thousand dollars, what would you do? You'd be gobsmacked. You would not stop talking about it. You would be so emotionally charged that you would tell your family, friends, and colleagues. You would *have* to talk about it. It's surprising, incredible, and absolutely joyous.

This is the "holy shit!" test: when something is so great, you are compelled to talk about it. Are your interactions with your clients, and the overall experience you create for them, passing the "holy shit!" test? If so, you've got a client for life.

"You Need to Hire Ben"

I want to conclude this chapter with one of the most powerful client experiences I've known. When I was an agent, I once had four listings in a neighborhood. It was a pretty great feeling: I would drive down the street and see these signs with my company logo on them. It felt good.

One day, I got a call from a woman. She must have seen these signs as well because she wanted to attend one of my open houses. But she was short with me—a little bit rude, to be honest. I told her the open house was over—she had missed it—and she turned even grumpier. So I decided *Fuck it*, and said, "Why don't you book a showing and I'll show you the house anyway, one on one?"

At that showing, she and I made a connection. It was clear she had had bad experiences with real estate agents before, and as a profession, she didn't trust us. Well, that explained her shortness. I discovered she was selling her home, without a real estate agent, as an FSBO. I offered to look at it for her. I didn't want to list it, but I said I could check if it was priced correctly and why it might not be selling.

This offer was genuine; I just wanted to help her. This is how I run my business. I priced her house and she ended up selling it on her own. I never made a dollar from helping her out like that.

But what I *did* get was a client. I began helping her search for houses to buy.

All the while, I got to know her. I asked her questions about herself and her family—not as an interview but because I genuinely wanted to connect with her. One day, she called me and asked whether her friend could come along and view houses with us. I said, *of course.* All three of us looked at properties, talked, and bonded.

At the end of that day, the two of them asked me to come into the kitchen for a chat. It turned out the friend was unhappy with her real estate agent and wanted to hire me. I would have loved to take her on as a client, but she was tied to another agent who had just sold her house, with a contract in place. There was nothing I could do.

The next week, the same friend was in the car with us again as we viewed houses. She said to me, "Ben, I'm a free agent now, so I can hire you."

Honestly, I was confused. What happened to her last agent? When I asked, she told me she had paid a $1,500 fee to break her contract with that agent—just so she could hire me to help her buy.

This is the power of connection. These are the lengths people will go to if they like you and believe you will do right by them. And most importantly, this is the power of the conversation behind your back. I didn't know this friend; she only heard about me from the woman I took on a showing. But that woman raved about me so much that this friend was willing to pay $1,500 to work with me.

Let me tell you, this happens more often than you would think. All without spending a cent on cold calling, drip mailing, or wrapping my logo on my car. I just care. I treat my clients as human beings with rich, full lives, like I wanted to be treated when I was a real estate investor. It makes all the difference.

Conclusion

When someone says "seven-figure business," most people think about making seven figures in one year. But I want you to challenge your thinking for a moment. Why do you need to hit that number in one year? Two hundred thousand dollars every year for five years is still a seven-figure business.

What is most valuable to you is not the money: it's the life you want. I hope that now, at the end of this book, you see that. Money is only the means. Growing your business is only the path. The destination is always the life you dream of.

So I challenge you to ask yourself, what do you want? What did you dream of when you got this license? Have you forgotten those dreams because you've been too busy? What do you want to do with your time? Is it more evenings with your family? Is it drinking tea in the morning without the pressure of a thousand phone calls? Is it having adventures and freedom?

Find out what you want and then chase it. Chase it today, not twenty years later or thirty or when you retire. Follow *your* dreams—not someone else's—and follow them *now*.

I'll be brutally honest with you: I don't care about the real estate industry. I only care about the people in it. Honestly, I don't give a shit about marketing and transactions and awards. All I care about is you using this real estate business to build the life you dream of. Because the truth is, if you understand this business correctly and leverage it in the right ways, it is an incredible tool for reaching your dreams. It is genuinely amazing. If you follow the steps in this book, you can make enough money to have a connection with your spouse and kids, carve out the vacations you want, and spend your time being the person you want to be. It's possible. This business gets you there.

But to do that, you need to stop chasing after real estate awards. You need to stop chasing after things someone told you you should want: an RV, a holiday home, an investment home that yields passive income. Everywhere I look, I see people walking around like zombies, running after everyone else's goals, and it kills me. As kids, no one asked us what we wanted. Now, as adults, we still don't know. We'll follow any path we see, desperately hoping that it takes us to where we want to go.

I'll tell you what I want. I want you to pause for a second and ask yourself, *what are my dreams?* I want you to get crystal fucking clear on your compass. Once you do, you can get out of your own way and build an amazing seven-figure business that pays for this life. You can travel. You can create memories with friends. You can make money while you sleep. You can make the business a servant to *you*, to your needs, not the other way around. You can stop being a hustler and become a business owner.

But to do that, you have to get out of your own way. Stop people pleasing. Stop being scared of conflict. Stop trying to make your parents happy and aiming for that shiny real estate award so you can believe you are valuable and worthy. Stop trying to put your best foot forward. It's time to just be yourself.

What Now?

This book is a concise explanation of processes that can help you discover the life you want and build a path to get there. But it doesn't operate on its own. As I've said a thousand times in this book, action is everything. Knowledge doesn't do much; you have to get off your ass and act.

I hope you're ready to do that. If you need more support, know that this book goes hand in hand with several of my coaching courses. If you're an agent and this book resonates with you, sign up for my Real Estate Reboot Camp. It packages all the systems in this book for you to execute immediately and be the change you want to see today. But honestly, those systems are a by-product, a bonus. The real value of the Real Estate Reboot Camp is the work you do on yourself. You'll learn to tackle your relationship with fear, how to conduct energy audits, how to hire, and how to overcome your personal challenges to achieve incredible growth. This personal coaching is the real 10X.

If you're a broker looking to change the game, then the Real Estate Reboot Camp is also for you. Several brokers now work with me to transform their agents from hustlers into business owners because they recognize that this industry is currently old, broken in some ways, and in need of a change. They want to shift the narrative. If you want to invest in the real retention of your agents, rather than discover just another sales technique, get in touch.

Alternately, if you've read this book and are less interested in the real estate process but are pumped about personal growth, come on one of my retreats. These are four-day deep dives where you leave your life behind, recharge, and rediscover yourself. I create a space to dig deeply into what you want. If you feel like you're not living as the fullest expression of yourself, then this retreat is what you need. By the end, you'll be energized and raring to go, but most importantly, you will have clarity. You will have set your compass and forged a path toward your goal. It's the catalyst for change.

Nor do you have to do the retreat alone. We've had agents who brought their whole team along. We've done father-son duos, mothers and daughters, husbands and wives. If there's a relationship you feel you need to work on, this is the space.

I trust that this book has helped you make some powerful mind-set shifts. Those shifts are valuable and the first step to achieving the life you want. But if you really want to put yourself under an intense microscope and discover the best version of yourself, then the Real Estate Reboot Camp and the retreats will take you far deeper. They will give you the insight and the accountability to massively reshape your life.

Ultimately, I'm looking for my tribe. If this book has resonated with you, the best place to go for further information is my website, benoosterveld.com. That's where you can learn more about my coaching programs, mindset retreats, and podcast. If you want to connect with me on social media, that's where you'll find the links, and if you're interested in booking me to speak, you can connect with me via the same website.

The Richest Real Estate Agent

What does it mean to be the richest real estate agent? It's not money. I know you think it is, but if you ask yourself why you want the money, you'll realize your goal is not the cash.

A real rich person is someone with amazing relationships and fewer worries. Their sense of security is not tied to money. They have a business that works *for* them, and they have the freedom to decide how much they dedicate to it. Maybe they want to work a ton of hours because they love their profession. Maybe they want to work only three hours a day. Either way, the richest real estate agent gets to choose.

That freedom to choose is everything. They can enjoy family vacations without being haunted by their cell phone on a beach. They can go on dates with their children, invest in their relationships, and spend time chasing their hobbies because the richest real estate agent is someone who has a team around them serving *their* vision of a life.

I want to conclude by sharing what makes *my* life rich. Ever since I was a kid, the coolest thing I could imagine was living life like I had a backstage pass. I wanted to find the secret doors, skip the lines at Disneyland, and be the guy the bouncer nodded at and waved straight in. I've already won the game on so many levels. I've built a business that makes me money while I'm sleeping and pays for the adventures I want. I have an incredible relationship with my wife and kids. And I still get a kick out of living life like I have a backstage pass. Those experiences inspire me far more than money.

You want to be the richest real estate agent? There's only one way to do that. Know what brings a sense of richness to your life and live it. Build a business around what you *really* want. Have the freedom to take holidays without bringing your laptop, spend time at your kid's sports game, and know the business is making money while you're gone. Create a life where you wake up every day happy. And if you can hook me up with an experience that feels like a backstage pass, hit me up. We should hang out.

www.ingramcontent.com/pod-product-compliance
Lightning Source LLC
Chambersburg PA
CBHW031850200326
41597CB00012B/355